STUFF EVERY
COFFEE LOVER
SHOULD KNOW

To my father, Rob—for all our
Saturday mornings at Kitchen
Emporium and for passing on
your love for coffee

Library of Congress Cataloging in Publication Number:
2020913049

ISBN: 978-68369-252-2

Printed in China

Typeset in Garamond, Agenda, and Sentinel

Designed by Ryan Hayes
Illustrations by Lucy Engelman
Production management by John J. McGurk

Quirk Books
215 Church Street
Philadelphia, PA 19106
quirkbooks.com

10 9 8 7 6 5 4 3 2

STUFF EVERY

COFFEE
LOVER

SHOULD KNOW

CANDACE ROSE
RARDON

QUIRK BOOKS
PHILADELPHIA

CONTENTS

COFFEE TRADITIONS ACROSS THE WORLD

SERVING COFFEE

RESOURCES

ACKNOWLEDGMENTS

INTRODUCTION

"The morning cup of coffee has an exhilaration about it which the cheering influence of the afternoon or evening cup of tea cannot be expected to reproduce."

—Oliver Wendell Holmes Sr.,
19th-century American physician and poet

Every day across the globe, approximately 1.6 billion cups of coffee are consumed. The United States alone is responsible for a quarter of that amount, and coffee is also the second most traded commodity in the world after oil. These are big stats and point to the tremendous role that coffee plays in our global economy. But as I've traveled the world over the past decade, I've also seen how important coffee is on the smallest, most human level.

I've been welcomed into family kitchens in Tamil Nadu, India, and was taught how to prepare rich creamy South Indian filter coffee. I've made new friends in some of Europe's oldest coffeeshops in Vienna and Paris, and sipped tiny Styrofoam cups of *tinto* in Cartagena, Colombia, which I always bought from a roving coffee vendor named Wilmet.

There's no question that coffee is one of the world's top drinks. Here are just a few of its most striking attributes.

Coffee is energizing. Each humble coffee bean holds over 1,000 chemical compounds, which give coffee its singular aroma and flavors. To coffee lovers, caffeine is often the most prized of these elements. Where would we be without our morning pick-me-up?

Coffee is evolving. Coffee has been consumed as a beverage for the past five or six hundred years. Compared to the 5,000-year history of tea, coffee seems pretty young. Some of the most popular manual brewing methods, such as the AeroPress and Hario V60, were invented as recently as the twenty-first century.

Coffee is global. Coffee isn't simply an essential part of cultures around the world. The physical journey that takes coffee from seed to cup is also extraordinary. The biggest coffee-drinking countries are not places where coffee is grown, so oceans and continents must be crossed for our esteemed brew to arrive in our cups.

Coffee is social. The specialty coffee industry honors this journey, with many roasters sourcing their coffee directly from growers, developing ongoing relationships with coffee farmers, and sharing their stories with customers. Relationships and stories—the very things coffee has been about since the beginning.

If you're reading this book, no doubt you and I already share a love for coffee. My hope is to help you discover an even greater appreciation for its nuanced flavors, complex history, and the role that we can play in bringing out the best in our beloved beverage.

COFFEE BASICS

WHAT IS COFFEE?

Many of the world's favorite drinks have legendary origin stories, and coffee is no exception. The discovery of coffee is dated to around 850 CE—and though there are numerous versions of the legend, they all center on a young goatherd in Ethiopia named Kaldi.

As the story goes, Kaldi's herd was normally calm and well behaved. But one day, he was amazed to see his goats dancing and leaping about as they feasted on bright red berries growing on the surrounding trees. When Kaldi tried the berries for himself, not only did he feel energized, but pretty soon he was dancing, too. Curious, he took a few berries to a local Sufi monastery. The abbot promptly declared the berries "the devil's work" and threw them into the fire. After a while, however, a delicious fragrance began emanating from the flames, so the monks rescued the newly roasted berries and immersed them in water—thus preparing the world's first cup of coffee.

The trees that Kaldi's goats found that fateful day in Ethiopia were none other than the tropical evergreen shrub now known as the *Coffea* plant. There are more than 120 *Coffea* species, but nearly all the coffee grown and consumed around the world is produced by just two: *Coffea arabica* and *Coffea canephora* (or, as it's better known, robusta).

Perhaps the most surprising fact to know about coffee is that it's a fruit! The drink is produced from the fruit of the *Coffea* tree, which is referred to as the coffee cherry. Because it's a fruit, you can technically eat coffee cherries, but the magic of coffee as we know it comes from the two seeds that grow *inside* each cherry—or what we call coffee "beans." Although Kaldi and his dancing goats ate the beans straight from the tree, today there's a lot more that happens before we enjoy our morning cup of joe. The six main steps in how coffee is made are:

GROWING	ROASTING
HARVESTING	GRINDING
PROCESSING	BREWING

We'll talk more about these steps soon, each of which is a world of its own. As you'll see, coffee has been an adventure from the very beginning—and though we now know much more about it than Kaldi did, there's still plenty for coffee lovers to discover and explore.

ANATOMY OF A COFFEE CHERRY

There's a lot going on inside a single coffee cherry—much more than just the two beans that typically grow in each one. Let's take a look at these layers.

Skin (exocarp): The outer skin of the cherry.

Pulp (mesocarp): Made up of water and sugar. Once the beans are removed, the leftover skins and pulp of the coffee cherry can be dried as Cascara (which comes from the Spanish for "husk") and brewed to make a tea-like infusion.

Mucilage (parenchyma): A viscous sugar-rich layer that covers each seed.

Parchment (endocarp): The paperlike hull around each bean.

Silver skin (spermoderm): An additional layer around each bean, which comes off during roasting (when it's referred to as "chaff").

Bean (endoderm): Most coffee cherries contain two beans (or seeds). However, 5% of cherries produce only one bean, known as a peaberry (see page 21).

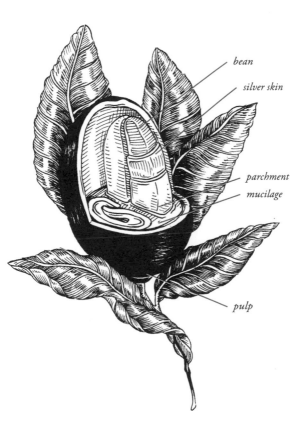

bean

silver skin

parchment

mucilage

pulp

HIGHLIGHTS FROM COFFEE HISTORY

"Coffee is a lot more than just a drink;
it's something happening."

—Gertrude Stein, *Selected Writings*

The story of coffee isn't remarkable only for what happened in the past. Indeed, innovations in how we produce and consume coffee are still happening today. Here's a look back at pivotal moments in coffee's evolution.

850 CE: As we know from the legend of Kaldi and his dancing goats (see page 10), coffee was discovered in Ethiopia. The presence of thousands of heirloom coffee varieties in the country lends even more truth to this apocryphal tale. It's also thought that the Ethiopian region of Kaffa is a possible origin of the English word *coffee*.

1400s: By this time, coffee has journeyed from Ethiopia to Yemen across the Red Sea. Yemen is the first country to cultivate coffee and open coffeehouses, and Sufi mystics use coffee to help them stay alert during evening prayers. The Arabic word for wine, *qahwa*, is also a likely origin of coffee's name.

1536: The Ottoman army invades Yemen, paving the way for coffee's arrival in Istanbul (and beyond). So swiftly do the Turks fall in love with coffee that a new position is created in the court of Suleiman the Magnificent: the *kahvecibaşı*—chief coffee maker for the sultan.

1600: Because of coffee's close ties with the Arab world, much of Europe is wary of it. But upon tasting coffee, Pope Clement VIII gives it his blessing, saying, "Why, this Satan's drink is so delicious that it would be a pity to let the infidels have exclusive use of it."

1670: On his way home to India from Mecca, a Sufi pilgrim named Baba Budan smuggles seven coffee seeds out of Yemen, bringing an end to the country's nearly 200-year monopoly on coffee.

1683: When the Ottoman army retreats after the Siege of Vienna, they leave everything behind—including 500 bags of coffee beans, which the Viennese assume is merely camel food. The only person who knows what they are is the Polish diplomat Georg Franz Kolschitzky (read more on page 106), who uses the beans to open one of Vienna's first coffeehouses, the Blue Bottle.

1700: Fifty years after the first coffeehouse was opened in England, some 2,000 coffeehouses serve London alone, providing meeting places for scholars, students, politicians, and people from all walks of life. The coffeehouses become known as "penny universities," after the cost of admission and a cup of coffee.

1723: A French naval officer named Gabriel de Clieu smuggles a coffee plant out of Louis XV's royal garden in Paris. After an arduous Atlantic crossing—during which de Clieu is said to have shared his own water ration with the plant because it needed "infinite care"—the seedling is successfully planted in Martinique, where de Clieu was stationed at the time. This isn't the first instance of coffee being brought to the Caribbean, but it's certainly the most noteworthy. It was a cultivated variety, or cultivar, of arabica known as Typica, and many say that 90% of the world's coffee plants today can be traced back to this single tree.

1773: Coffee is slow to catch on in the American colonies—but that all changes with the Boston Tea Party. As John Adams writes to his wife, "Tea must be universally renounced," and Boston's Green Dragon coffeehouse and tavern is dubbed the "headquarters of the Revolution."

Mid-1800s: The founding of Pioneer Steam Coffee and Spice Mills (what will later become Folgers) in 1850 is considered one of the starting points of the first wave of coffee. Coffee industry professionals use the designations *first*, *second*, and *third wave* to represent a distinct paradigm of how coffee is produced and consumed, and the first wave is all about coffee as a mass commodity. The quality of coffee is low as suppliers race to meet global demand.

1860s: If the Revolutionary War piqued the taste for coffee in the United States, the Civil War only serves to cement it. Each Union soldier receives an annual ration of 36 pounds of coffee beans; some rifle stocks even feature a built-in coffee grinder.

1884: Angelo Moriondo invents the world's first espresso machine in Turin, Italy.

1907: U.S. President Theodore Roosevelt drinks a cup of Maxwell House coffee in Nashville. He is said to have proclaimed, "Good to the last drop," which later becomes the brand's legendary slogan.

1938: Instant coffee has been around since the late 1700s, but Nestlé's launch of Nescafé introduces a new method of making soluble coffee, which soon becomes a staple for U.S. soldiers in World War II.

1952: Just as diamond engagement rings were the result of a marketing campaign, the coffee break is invented by the Pan American Coffee Bureau to promote coffee consumption.

1966: Dutch American coffee roaster Alfred Peet opens Peet's Coffee & Tea in Berkeley, California, which is now viewed as the start of the second wave of coffee.

1971: Starbucks is founded in Seattle. After Howard Schultz's famed trip to Italy in 1983 (see page 60 for more), the company is credited with bringing coffeehouse culture and specialty espresso drinks to the U.S., along with a renewed focus on quality coffee. However, coffee's second wave is more about the experience of cafés, as opposed to the coffee itself.

2002: Coffee professional Trish Rothgeb coins the term "third-wave coffee" in an article for the Specialty Coffee Association. The hallmarks of this era include direct trade with farmers, single-origin coffee, and lighter roasts that honor the unique flavors of each origin, as well as the rise of independent coffee roasters during the 1990s, such as Portland's Stumptown and Chicago's Intelligentsia. Ultimately, third-wave coffee puts the focus back on the art and craft of brewing.

TERMS EVERY COFFEE LOVER SHOULD KNOW

Acidity: A positive feeling of crisp, fruity brightness in coffee, created by over 30 different acids. Lighter roasts tend to have greater acidity than darker roasts.

Arabica: One of two main species of the *Coffea* plant. It is valued for its high quality and complex flavors and accounts for 75% of global coffee production.

Blend: A mixture of coffee beans from multiple origins. The purpose of a blend is to create a consistent, well-balanced taste, as opposed to highlighting the unique terroir of a single origin.

Bloom: An important step in many manual brewing methods. It involves pouring water over the coffee grounds, which helps release carbon dioxide and kick-start the extraction (see page 75).

Body: The perceived consistency and texture of coffee on the tongue, often described as light, medium, or heavy. Other descriptors include creamy, buttery, silky, juicy, and thin.

Caffeine: Natural compound and stimulant found in the coffee plant. Robusta beans have nearly twice as much caffeine as arabica varieties.

Commodity coffee: Term that describes low-grade, low-priced coffee that is traded on the New York Coffee Exchange and typically used for instant coffee and blends.

Cupping: A method for preparing and tasting multiple coffees, used by coffee professionals to score specialty coffee.

Direct trade: The practice of sourcing coffee directly from growers, instead of using importers or other intermediaries. It emphasizes long-term relationships between farmers and roasters and pays higher, more ethical prices for higher-quality coffee.

Dry aroma: The scent of dry ground coffee as it releases volatile compounds; also known as the fragrance.

Espresso: Italian for "pressed out," this term refers to a method of preparing coffee using extreme pressure. It is also the name of a particular drink, known for its highly concentrated flavors and rich body.

Extraction: The process in which coffee's soluble compounds dissolve in water during brewing, which give it flavor and aroma. An underextraction doesn't dissolve enough flavor and leads to sour coffee; by contrast, overextracted coffee is excessively bitter. Two of the most common ways of extracting coffee manually are *immersion*, in which grounds are immersed in water through the entire extraction, and *pour-over* (or *drip*), in which water is poured over grounds and gravity draws the water down through the coffee into the vessel below.

Flavor: The taste of brewed coffee, which should always include a balance of acidity, sweetness, and bitterness.

Green coffee: Term used to describe raw coffee beans—which are pale green—that have been processed but not yet roasted.

Peaberry: A natural mutation in which a coffee cherry produces only one bean, not two. They are often smaller and rounder than regular coffee beans, and so should be separated and roasted on their own to ensure an even, consistent roast. Peaberries are typically sold as their own blend (e.g., Tanzanian peaberry coffee).

Processing: The step of removing coffee beans from each cherry. There are several processing methods, which happen in the producing country before green coffee is exported (see page 26).

Roasting: A process that uses heat to transform raw coffee beans—not only do they change in color from green to brown, but various chemical reactions unlock coffee's aroma and flavors.

Robusta: One of two main species of the *Coffea* plant. It is considered inferior to arabica because of its harsh, bitter flavor, but it is also cheaper to produce and more resistant to pests and disease.

Single origin: Term used to describe coffee grown in one geographic region. It can be as broad as several producers in the same country and as specific as a single farm, estate, or cooperative.

Specialty coffee: The Specialty Coffee Association defines specialty-grade coffee as that which receives 80+ points on a 100-point tasting scale. This term also refers to a broader mindset that views coffee as a unique product, not a mass commodity. It values sourcing quality single-origin coffee, using sustainable growing practices, and paying ethical prices to coffee farmers and growers.

Strength: The intensity of a coffee's taste, determined by the proportion (or brew ratio) of coffee grounds to water used during brewing.

Variety: A subset or type of a larger species of the *Coffea* plant, either natural or human-made; it is often used interchangeably with varietal and cultivar, or a cultivated variety.

Wet aroma: The scent of brewed coffee, also known simply as the aroma.

HOW COFFEE IS MADE

"Coffee you develop, and by skill and judgment change from caterpillar to a butterfly, as it were—you bring out a hidden treasure."

—Jabez Burns, 19th-century English pioneer in roasting coffee

From the moment a ripe coffee cherry is picked, coffee goes on a pretty incredible journey before it reaches our mugs. Here's an overview of the six key steps in how coffee is made, with a focus on the steps that take place in the producing country.

Growing

Coffee is grown around the world, but there are certain regions where coffee plants thrive: between the Tropic of Cancer and the Tropic of Capricorn, in a special zone along the equator known as the "Bean Belt." This area offers the following key features.

Tropical climate: The ideal climate for growing coffee has hot, humid days; cold nights (but no frost or freezing temperatures); and generous rainfall.

Elevation: Within the Bean Belt, mountainous regions are prized, especially those above 4,000 feet.

At higher elevations, coffee beans have to work harder to mature—and the longer a bean takes to ripen, the more time it has for delicious, complex sugars to develop. A good rule of thumb is higher elevation equals higher quality.

Fertile soil: Soil has a huge influence on coffee's flavor. Much of the world's best coffee is grown in volcanic soil, which is rich in minerals and nutrients.

The term *terroir* (from the French, meaning "a sense of place") is familiar in the world of oenology, referring to the many factors that influence a wine's character. But it's just as relevant to coffee. Everything that happens around the coffee plant will find its way into the final drink—from the weather and soil to the biodiversity on the farm.

> **Tip:** Many specialty-coffee packages will list the elevation at which the beans were grown, as well as other designations. Mexico uses the term *Altura* ("height"); Papua New Guinea has "Mile High"; and farms across Central America state HB and SHB, which stand for "hard bean" (for coffee grown above 3,000 feet) and "strictly hard bean" (grown above 4,500 feet).

Arabica vs. Robusta: A Comparison

Let's take a closer look at the two most important species of the *Coffea* plant.

~~~~~~

Robusta (*Coffea canephora*)

Robusta accounts for around 25% of the world's coffee production. True to its name, it's robust and less susceptible to pests and diseases than arabica. It matures quickly and is highly productive; each tree yields 2 to 3 pounds of green coffee (beans that have been processed but not yet roasted) a year. Robusta also contains twice as much caffeine as arabica, which contributes to its harsh, bitter flavor. It's therefore considered inferior and is often used for instant coffee and blends.

Arabica (*Coffea arabica*)

Arabica accounts for 75% of global coffee production. It's more expensive to cultivate, more sensitive to threats, and yields only about half the amount of green coffee as robusta. Because it's grown at higher elevations, arabica coffee is sweeter and more acidic than robusta. It is celebrated for its complex flavors, which include notes of chocolate, caramel, fruits, and berries. When it comes to quality coffee, arabica beans set the bar high.

~~~~~~

Harvesting

Like strawberries, coffee cherries don't all ripen at the same time—and they stop ripening as soon as they're picked. So, coffee must be picked by hand (although some mechanization has been adopted on larger farms, especially in Brazil). Hand harvesting is challenging, labor-intensive work, because pickers need to return to the same plant several times as the cherries ripen. Here's a look at the two main harvesting methods.

Strip picking: As the name suggests, this method involves stripping an entire branch of its cherries—not just the fully ripe ones—and sorting them later. Green and partially ripe cherries are discarded or used for lower-grade coffee.

Selective picking: In this method, pickers harvest coffee cherries singly, choosing only ripe red cherries. Selective picking is time-consuming and thus comes with a higher price tag; it is used for high-quality coffee.

Processing

After the coffee cherries have been picked, they're still not yet ready to be roasted. First, they need to be processed, and in the world of coffee, the word "process" refers to a specific step: when the beans are removed from each cherry. There are three main processing methods, and each has a noticeable effect on the coffee's flavor.

Natural/dry process: This method is the simplest and most traditional. The cherries are spread out to dry in the sun; after several weeks, a machine separates the bean from the dried fruit. Because the beans spend so much time with the pulp still attached, they often absorb extra sweetness and fruity notes—but they can also take on unpleasant, earthy flavors. Natural processing doesn't require a lot of infrastructure or irrigation, so it's a good option in those parts of the world with limited access to water.

Washed/wet process: Coffee cherries pass through a pulping machine, which removes the skin and pulp from the beans. Next, the thin, sticky layer of mucilage is removed before the beans are dried, either in the sun or by machine. Though washed processing is more expensive than natural processing, it is the preferred method for specialty coffee. With this method you'll get all of the delicate flavors and aromas that the beans have to give, rather than obscuring them with fruity notes from the pulp.

Semiwashed: This final method is a hybrid of the first two. As with washed processing, the coffee cherries are pulped, but the beans are then laid out to dry with their mucilage still attached, similar to natural processing (another name for this method is pulped natural process). The resulting flavors are a hybrid as well, with some of the sweetness you find in dry processing and some of the cleaner notes characteristic of the wet process. Semiwashed processing is often used in Indonesia, where it's called wet hold (or *Giling Basah*), and across Latin America, where it's known as the honey (or *miel*) process.

Roasting

It's technically safe to eat raw coffee beans (and you'll get a caffeine buzz, too), but they're so hard and dense, it wouldn't be very safe for your teeth—or your grinding machine. That's where roasting comes in, which transforms the beans' texture and taste.

Roasting is both a science and an art. It requires precision and a grasp of thermodynamics, yet it's also intensely personal; two roasters might have two very different opinions on how to roast a particular coffee. Most roasters start out with the same tool—a drum roaster, which has a heated rotating cylinder—and they work with the same two variables: temperature and time. As soon as the beans start heating up, a variety of processes is kicked off.

Evaporation: Green coffee beans are dense beasts, but thanks to moisture evaporating, they lose about 15% to 20% of their weight during roasting.

Maillard reaction: While the beans are lightening up weight-wise as they roast, they're growing darker in color because of a chemical reaction. You may not recognize it by name, but you've undoubtedly seen the Maillard reaction at work: just as a steak turns brown as it cooks, so too do roasting coffee beans.

Caramelization of sugar: Remember all those complex sugars we love in coffee? Now's the time when they start to caramelize inside the beans and develop serious flavor.

First crack: At last, it's time for the grand finale. All these reactions are leading up to the big moment—a physical crack that you can very much hear, just as if you were making popcorn. It signals a great release of carbon dioxide and heat, which causes the beans to double in size. It also opens up the coffee beans, so they won't be as dense as they were before.

Roasters will either remove the beans after the first crack (for light and medium roasts) or keep cooking them until a second crack sounds (for dark roasts). There are three main levels of roasting, which are associated with common roast names:

Light: cinnamon roast, light city roast, half city roast

Medium: American roast, breakfast roast, city roast

Dark: espresso roast, French roast, Italian roast, New Orleans roast, Vienna roast

Lighter roasts highlight the original character and flavors of the coffee, whereas darker roasts feature what's known as the *roast character*—that is, notes imparted by further roasting, which are often chocolatey and nutty.

After roasting, it's time to cool the beans as quickly as possible and pack 'em up.

> **Tip:** Want to roast your own beans at home? Check out companies such as Sweet Maria's, which sells green coffee and home roasting machines (sweetmarias.com).

Grinding and Brewing

The first three steps in how coffee is made—growing, harvesting, and processing—take place in the producing country, and often on the very farm where the beans were harvested. The last two steps should ideally take place where the coffee will be consumed—because when it comes to grinding and brewing coffee beans, coffee lovers have a lot of control over the final product. We'll dive into the importance of grinding your own coffee in the coming entries, and an entire chapter has been devoted to the craft of brewing better coffee at home (see "Brewing Methods," page 67).

FRESHNESS IN COFFEE

Freshness is everything with coffee, particularly in the world of specialty coffee. Unlike wine, coffee doesn't improve with age—it just gets old. To ensure your coffee is fresh, there are three dates to pay particular attention to.

Harvesting: If it's stored properly, green coffee can stay fresh for up to 12–18 months—beyond that, it begins to age, losing intensity and flavor. Specialty roasters such as Intelligentsia often list the harvest date on the coffee package.

Roasting: After coffee beans are roasted, their window of freshness is 2–3 weeks, so try not to buy more than you'll consume in that timeframe. The roast date is another key detail you can expect to find listed on bags of specialty coffee. As the coffee site *Perfect Daily Grind* suggests, "Treat buying coffee like buying bread: only buy enough for a week or so."

Grinding: As we'll talk more about on page 32, freshly ground coffee is a thing of fleeting beauty. Some say it loses its freshness after mere moments, others say after 15 minutes, but the general consensus is that within a half hour, ground coffee is stale.

WHOLE BEAN
VS. GROUND COFFEE

As coffee lovers, there's a lot we can do to improve the quality of our coffee at home, but the two biggest game-changers are (1) buying whole coffee beans and (2) grinding them right before we brew.

Coffee beans are small but mighty—each tiny bean holds over 1,000 chemical compounds. To many of us, the most important of those elements is caffeine, but dozens of other compounds are responsible for coffee's incredible aroma and flavors. Moreover, these compounds are volatile, which means they easily evaporate. (The Middle English root of *volatile* means "creature that flies," which is exactly how we might think of the delicate compounds inside our coffee.)

And therein lies the power of whole coffee beans: as long as the beans are whole, all those aromatic compounds are safely protected inside. But as soon as coffee is ground and exposed to oxygen, an invisible seal of freshness is broken. Some say that ground coffee loses 60% of its aroma just 15 minutes after grinding. By grinding coffee right when we're about to brew, its aroma and flavors will have less time to evaporate, and there will be more delicious compounds for us to extract during brewing. But grinding whole beans in the moment isn't only about maximizing the freshness of our coffee; it also gives us more control over grind size, which is one of the most important variables in manual brewing (see page 68).

When we grind our own coffee, not only can we make sure that the coffee grounds are the right size for our chosen brewing device and method, but we also have the ability to make adjustments to our brewing process. Sometimes, even the smallest tweak in grind size can have a big effect on the taste of our coffee.

Tip: To see what a difference grinding coffee beans in the moment can make, compare the fragrance of freshly ground coffee to beans ground an hour earlier. Better yet, brew a cup of coffee with each set of grounds and note how their flavor profiles differ.

Choosing the Right Coffee Grinder

Generally, there are two types of grinders that you can use to grind whole beans at home.

Blade grinder

Like a blender or food processor, this grinder works by chopping up coffee beans using a single blade. The good news about blade grinders is that they're simple and inexpensive; the bad news is that they typically result in an inconsistent grind, with fine and coarse particles mixed together. Because coarser grounds take longer to extract, an uneven grind leads to an uneven brew.

Burr grinder

Instead of a single blade, this grinder has two rotating blades, or burrs, between which the beans are crushed and ground, rather than chopped. A wheel burr grinder has two flat round blades, whereas a cone burr grinder has two conical blades, one inside the other. The amount of space between the wheels or cones can be adjusted and determines the size of the grind—the closer together they are, the finer the beans will be ground. Burr grinders produce a much more uniform grind, so they're the preferred choice of coffee professionals.

TYPES OF COFFEE

*"The powers of a man's mind are
directly proportioned to the quantity
of coffee he drinks."*

—Sir James Mackintosh,
18th- and 19th-century Scottish politician

For most of history, whole bean coffee was the only type of coffee there was. Consumers would roast and grind it themselves at home. In the past century, however, alternative types of coffee have risen to fame, winning over fans with their convenience and speed.

Preground coffee

San Francisco-based Hills Brothers Coffee was the first to market the vacuum pack in 1900. Their ads promised that coffee would "Keep Fresh Forever If Seal Is Unbroken," and the demand for preroasted coffee beans took off. Preground coffee was soon to follow, but as we covered in the previous entry, it is often stale by the time it's purchased and just can't compete with the rich aroma and complex flavors of freshly ground coffee.

Instant coffee

Also known as soluble coffee, instant coffee has been around in some form since the late eighteenth century. But in 1938, Nestlé launched Nescafé, which became a staple of soldiers during World War II and, soon after, of American families in the 1950s, who were all about new convenient food products, from TV dinners to frozen juice concentrates.

Instant coffee isn't just easy to make—it's also cheap, it has a longer shelf life than fresh beans, and for those on the run, it's quick (no burr grinders or brew ratios needed here). Indeed, one of the only cons of instant coffee is its quality, considered subpar because it has historically been made from low-grade robusta. However, companies such as Voilà Coffee and Swift Cup have recently been raising the standard, pioneering an innovation on instant known as microground coffee, which is a combination of finely ground arabica beans and specialty instant coffee. The result: no sacrificing quality for convenience.

Coffee capsules

Swiss inventor and Nestlé employee Éric Favre is known as the "father of capsule coffee." In 1986, Nestlé released his design for the first Nespresso capsule machine. Company executives had their eye on offices and hotels as their target market, but single-serving capsule machines are now commonly found in homes as well.

Like instant coffee, capsules are quick and simple to use, and if you're entertaining a crowd, the sheer variety of available styles and flavors will help you cater to each individual's taste. But there are a number of drawbacks: capsules are expensive—for the same price (or even less), you could be buying top-shelf whole beans—and they lock you into a particular brand (many capsules work only with a specific system). Most important, they create a tremendous amount of waste, since the majority of disposable capsules are not recyclable.

> **Tip:** If you already own a capsule machine, look into purchasing reusable, refillable pods. Not only are they friendlier to the environment, they can also be filled with your own quality, freshly ground coffee.

THE TASTE OF COFFEE

"How sweet coffee tastes!
Lovelier than a thousand kisses . . ."
—Johann Sebastian Bach, *Coffee Cantata*

The best-tasting coffee should have four key components—and even more important, they all need to be in balance. For instance, the longer coffee beans are roasted, the lower their acidity and the greater their bitterness.

Acidity: If you've ever described a cup of coffee as bright, crisp, or even zingy, you've picked up on its acidity. There are more than thirty different acids in coffee, including malic acid, phosphoric acid, and citric acid (the same acid found in oranges and lemons). Acidity is prized in coffee—think of it more like biting into a tangy green apple than a lip-puckering lemon.

Sweetness: The inherent natural sweetness found in coffee is a subtle, but important, flavor sensation—it helps round out the acidity. Lighter roasts tend to offer a fruity sweetness (think strawberries or grapes), whereas darker roasts feature notes of chocolate, caramel, and honey.

Bitterness: Given that caffeine itself is bitter, coffee inherently has a certain level of bitterness—if it isn't bitter, it isn't coffee! However, there's a good level of bitter notes, and then there's negative bitterness. This unpleasant sharpness can especially happen during roasting—any burnt notes of smoke or carbon can generally be attributed to overroasting.

Body: Body isn't a taste, per se, but rather something you can feel in your entire mouth—hence this characteristic is often referred to as *mouthfeel*. Body is the consistency and texture of coffee on the tongue, be it heavy or light, creamy or thin.

The best coffee is complex coffee. We want coffee that tells us a story in the cup—with some notes emerging at first, followed by other notes as the aroma develops. Rather than tasting dull or flat, coffee should take us on a captivating journey of flavor and sensation.

Note: Professional coffee tastings are known as *cuppings*. See "How to Host a Coffee Cupping," on page 130, for all you need to know on this topic.

COFFEE GROWING REGIONS

"Coffee is a language in itself."

—**Jackie Chan,** 20th- and 21st-century
martial artist and film star

Specialty coffee is all about stories—not just the story of flavors and aromas in your cup, but the stories of everyone who helped it evolve from seed to drink. The Specialty Coffee Association identifies several key roles in the world of coffee, including the green coffee buyer, the roaster, and the barista. But at the beginning of every coffee's journey is the person without whom the rest of the process simply wouldn't be possible: the farmer.

Today, 125 million people in over seventy countries rely on coffee production for their livelihood. The specialty coffee industry makes it a priority to honor the work of these farmers and growers—not only by paying them higher, more sustainable prices, but also by helping consumers discover the unique flavors of each origin. From the highlands of Ethiopia to the volcanic slopes of Costa Rica, the diversity of coffee origins could fill an entire book—and indeed they have, such as James Hoffman's *The World Atlas of Coffee*. Here's a brief tour of the main growing regions across the globe.

Africa

Ever since Kaldi's dancing goats discovered coffee beans (see page 10), Ethiopia has stayed true to its roots as the birthplace of coffee. Not only is it still one of the top producers (as of 2020, it ranked fifth in the world), but it is one of only three countries that arabica coffee is native to (as well as parts of Kenya and Sudan). Throughout this entry, we'll touch on arabica varieties associated with each region—which are subsets of the larger arabica species—but perhaps none are as fascinating as Ethiopian heirlooms. Ethiopia is home to nearly 10,000 native varieties of coffee trees, which grow together in wild coffee forests. Only about a thousand have been identified, so they're generally sold under the umbrella term *heirloom varieties*.

While Ethiopia is a testament to coffee's heritage, other African producers are helping advance the future of coffee. Coffee arrived in Kenya only in 1893, but the country is now known for its coffee research. It has created several drought- or disease-resistant varieties of arabica, from SL28 and SL34 to Ruiru 11, developed by Kenya's Coffee Research Institute in 1985.

Popular growing countries: Burundi, Democratic Republic of the Congo, Ethiopia, Kenya, Malawi, Rwanda, Tanzania, Uganda

Common arabica varieties: Ethiopian heirlooms, SL28, SL34, Ruiru 11, Bourbon (see page 46)

Processing: Natural and washed processing

Flavor profiles: Fruity, floral notes with citric acidity. Coffee from the Yirgacheffe region of Ethiopia offers notes of Earl Grey tea, and Kenya's SL28 variety is prized for its black currant flavor.

Arabian Peninsula

Even though the Arabian Peninsula is home to only one coffee-producing country—Yemen—it has played such a notable role in the history of coffee that it more than deserves its own section. Coffee most likely made its way from Ethiopia to Yemen in the thirteenth or fourteenth century, either on trade missions across the Red Sea or with pilgrims en route to Mecca.

Ethiopia may be the birthplace of coffee, but Yemen holds a different honor: it is the first country that produced coffee as a commercial crop. For nearly 200 years, until the end of the seventeenth century, Yemen was the world's only supplier of coffee. A number of factors have since limited its supply, from an ongoing civil war to the fact that only 3% of its arid land is suitable for agriculture. Even still, Yemeni coffee remains highly sought after, and is often considered the rarest coffee in the world.

Popular growing countries: Yemen

Common arabica varieties: Heirloom varieties similar to those in Ethiopia

Processing: Yemen's dry climate means that all its coffee is grown on terraces and undergoes natural processing, often on the rooftops of farmers' homes.

Flavor profiles: Wine-like acidity, with notes of chocolate and dried fruit

> **Note:** In the past, Yemeni coffee always passed through the port city of Mocha, or Al-Mokha, before it was exported. The port was so important that Yemeni coffee became known as Mocha (not to be confused with the chocolatey drink discussed on page 65).

Asia

For years, Yemen went to great lengths to protect its monopoly on coffee; all beans marked for export were boiled or partially roasted first, so that they would be unable to germinate (which would allow other countries to grow coffee for themselves). That all changed in 1670, when a Sufi pilgrim named Baba Budan, on his way home to India from Mecca, smuggled seven raw coffee seeds out of Yemen by taping them to his stomach (seven is a holy number in Islam). He then planted the seeds in the hills of southern India, where they instantly flourished. The coffee-growing region of Baba Budangiri is named in his honor.

A couple decades later, in 1696, the Dutch governor of Malabar (present-day Kochi, India) sent some coffee seedlings as a gift to his counterpart in Jakarta (then known as Batavia). By 1711 Indonesia was exporting coffee to Europe via the Dutch East India Company, and today it is still the fourth-largest coffee-producing country in the world.

Popular growing countries: India, Indonesia, Myanmar, Papua New Guinea, Vietnam

Common arabica varieties: Typica, Bourbon, and Timor Hybrid (also known as Tim Tim, this is a naturally occurring cross between arabica and robusta).

Processing: Indonesia is distinctive for its semiwashed process known as wet hulling, or *Giling Basah* (see page 28).

Flavor profiles: The wet-hulled method gives Indonesian coffees low acidity, strong body, and flavor notes such as earthy, smoky, spicy, and woody.

South America

Coffee's spread through the Americas is also rife with intrigue. After Gabriel de Clieu's smuggled Typica seedling arrived in Martinique (see page 16), coffee made its way to nearby colonies such as French Guiana—and it's there that another act of coffee espionage took place. In 1727, the Portuguese were eager to start growing coffee in Brazil, but they couldn't get hold of any plants. So when Brazilian officer Francisco de Melo Palheta was sent to French Guiana to help sort out a border dispute, legend says that he also seduced the wife of the governor. Upon his departure, she gave him a bouquet; hidden among the flowers were none other than a few cuttings of *Coffea arabica*.

By the mid-1800s, Brazil had overtaken Indonesia as the global coffee powerhouse—but at the expense of deforestation and the enslavement of a huge number of people. Brazil has been the top coffee producer ever since, singlehandedly growing a third of the world's supply; neighboring Colombia is the third-largest producer.

Popular growing countries: Bolivia, Brazil, Peru, Colombia, Ecuador

Common arabica varieties: Typica, Caturra, Castillo

Processing: Colombian coffee tends to be washed, whereas Brazil uses natural processing. Coffee in Brazil tends to be grown at lower altitudes than in Colombia and other South American countries (remember that high altitude leads to high acidity and sweetness), so the dry method helps impart more flavor to the bean.

Flavor profiles: Brazilian coffee is known for its low acidity and heavy body, which makes it a popular base for espresso blends.

Central America

After centuries of smuggling, coffee suddenly became a lot more accessible in the nineteenth century. When Costa Rica declared independence from Spain in 1821, the government was keen to develop coffee as a cash crop, so officials handed out free coffee seeds to farmers and even provided plots of land for growing them. In 1868, the Guatemalan government also gave away a million coffee seedlings, to replace indigo as the country's primary cash crop.

Most of these seeds were of the Typica variety, but this period also saw the arrival of a new arabica variety: Bourbon (pronounced "boor-BOHN"). Why the French-sounding name? Because it was grown by the French on the island of Bourbon (now Réunion) in the Indian Ocean. Over time, the Typica coffee they originally planted naturally mutated into a new variety. The Bourbon cultivar was introduced to Brazil in 1860 and soon made its way north, producing coffee with bright acidity, pleasant sweetness, and chocolatey notes—all of which are still hallmarks of Central American coffees today.

Popular growing countries: Costa Rica, El Salvador, Guatemala, Honduras, Nicaragua, Panama

Common arabica varieties: Typica, Bourbon, Pacamara, Geisha (see "Renowned Coffee Varieties," page 48)

Processing: Many coffees in Central America are washed, leading to bright, clean flavors; Costa Rica developed the semiwashed method known as the honey process.

Flavor profiles: Well-balanced, with notes of chocolate, caramel, honey, nuts, and fruit

Note: Most of North America lies well above the Bean Belt, but a few key coffee-growing regions in this part of the world include Hawaii, southern Mexico, and Jamaica in the Caribbean.

Renowned Coffee Varieties

There are myriad varieties of arabica coffee—both natural and human-made hybrids—but a few standouts are worth sampling if you have the opportunity. Here are some top varieties that also command top-dollar prices.

Hawaiian Kona

Hawaii's Big Island offers more than just picture-postcard views; its active volcanoes contribute to a perfect micro-climate for growing coffee. Afternoon cloud cover and rich volcanic soil help create a smooth, aromatic coffee with mild acidity. Hawaii is also the only coffee-producing region in a developed country.

Jamaica Blue Mountain

The misty Blue Mountains in eastern Jamaica present another unique microclimate for growing coffee. Like Hawaiian Kona, this sought-after variety is smooth and clean, with floral tones and hardly any bitterness.

Panama Geisha

Perhaps most deserving of the hype—and high price—is the Geisha variety, especially that grown in Panama's Boquete region. It's prized for complex, citrusy flavors and a tea-like body, and it can't seem to stop breaking its own sales records. In 2019, a single pound of specialty Geisha beans sold at auction for $1,029! (For comparison, green commodity-grade coffee often sells for just $1 to $2 per pound.)

CAFFEINE CONTENT 101

"I never laugh until I've had my coffee."
—**Clark Gable**, 20th-century American film star

Morning jolt. Liquid energy. Cupped lightning. There's a plethora of nicknames for coffee, most of them referring to its most prized natural compound. Here are a few things that can influence just how much caffeine your coffee holds.

Robusta vs. arabica: Robusta has nearly twice as much caffeine as arabica. Caffeine is naturally bitter, which helps explain the harsh notes and bitterness associated with robusta coffee beans.

High vs. low elevation: Caffeine is a natural pesticide designed to help the coffee plant defend itself. Because coffee plants grown at high altitudes face fewer threats, they will generally have less caffeine than low-elevation plants.

Espresso vs. drip coffee: A common myth is that espresso has more caffeine than brewed coffee—and taken ounce for ounce, that's true. Espresso has 40–60mg of caffeine per ounce, compared to brewed coffee's 12–21mg/ounce. However, we also have to consider standard serving sizes. A double shot of espresso is just 2 ounces, but a cup of drip coffee may be 8–12 ounces—or more, if you're sipping on a venti from Starbucks.

Light vs. dark roast: The lighter the roast, the more caffeine—or so says another common coffee myth, based on the idea that caffeine is "burned off" with heat. As it turns out, caffeine is quite stable during the roasting process. So on a bean-by-bean basis, there isn't a big difference between the caffeine in light and dark roasts. However . . .

Volume vs. weight: . . . light and dark roasts *can* have differing amounts of caffeine, depending on how coffee is measured. As coffee is roasted and water evaporates, the beans grow larger in size but lighter in mass. So if we measure coffee by volume, lighter roasts will have a bit more caffeine; since their beans are denser but smaller, we'll need more beans to have the same volume as dark-roasted coffee (and more beans means more caffeine). Measuring coffee by weight means the opposite is true. Even though dark-roasted beans are larger, they weigh less, so you need more of them to equal the weight of light-roasted coffee.

How Decaf Coffee Is Made

Several methods for decaffeinating coffee have been developed since the nineteenth century. They all work with coffee beans while they're green (i.e., before roasting), but some processes use chemical solvents to extract caffeine; not only is this potentially harmful to consumers, it can also affect a coffee's flavor. Look for decaf coffee that was processed by one of the following methods—and keep in mind that it is never completely free of caffeine (the USDA defines decaf as 97% caffeine free).

Carbon Dioxide Process

This recently developed method uses highly pressurized carbon dioxide to draw out caffeine molecules from coffee beans. It is less toxic than other methods but expensive, so it's generally used only on large quantities of commodity-grade coffee.

Swiss Water Process

Instead of chemicals or solvents, this process used by the Swiss Water decaf coffee company extracts caffeine naturally using the innate power of osmosis. You can learn much more on the company's website (swisswater.com), but the important thing to know is that it is the only certified organic method for decaffeinating coffee. Therefore, it is the preferred choice of specialty coffeeshops and small-batch roasters.

CAFFEINE COMPARISON CHART

To see just how strong a cup of joe is, let's take a look at common coffee drinks and other popular caffeinated beverages, with their approximate caffeine contents.

DRINK	CAFFEINE CONTENT PER 8 OZ. SERVING (UNLESS NOTED)
Decaf coffee	2–12mg
Coca-Cola	21mg
Diet Coke	28mg
Green tea	35–45mg
Espresso	60mg/ounce
Instant coffee	62mg
Red Bull	80mg
Brewed coffee	95–165mg
Starbucks nitro cold brew	140mg

HOW TO STORE COFFEE

As beloved as it is, coffee has a lot of enemies, from oxygen and moisture to light and heat. Here's a closer look at how—and how *not*—to keep your coffee fresh.

Keep it dark and dry: Store your coffee in a dark, dry place, such as a pantry or cupboard away from a stove or heat source. Whether you keep your coffee in its original packaging or another opaque, airtight container, make sure it has a one-way degassing valve, which releases carbon dioxide without letting air in.

Avoid the chill chest: A popular myth says that storing coffee in your refrigerator or freezer will keep it fresh for longer. However, both environments create moisture, and when you take out the coffee to room temperature, further condensation will form inside the container. Humid coffee goes bad almost instantly.

Beware of odors: Coffee is porous, which is why coffee grounds are often used to neutralize bad odors. If your storage container isn't completely closed, its contents will absorb the odors around it, especially in a fridge. That's not what we're looking for in our specialty coffee!

A NOTE ABOUT WATER QUALITY

A cup of coffee is 90% to 99% water, so it's important to talk about the water we're using. Before you brew, follow these tips.

The trouble with tap: Tap water is high in chlorine, which can mask flavors in coffee. Before using tap water to brew, make sure it has no odors of chlorine or noticeable impurities.

Minerals matter: The right minerals in water (such as magnesium, calcium, and bicarbonate) help extract a better balance of flavors from coffee beans. Companies such as Third Wave Water sell packets of minerals that are ideal for brewing coffee. Distilled water that hasn't been treated with minerals will lead to an overly acidic or sour flavor, and hard mineral water may extract too many bitter notes.

Note: Hard mineral water can lead to limescale buildup in kettles and brewing devices. A little routine maintenance using white vinegar or a descaler can help keep your equipment in tip-top shape.

Invest in a filter: A pitcher-style charcoal filter can also help remove impurities before brewing.

COFFEE ACCESSORIES

"I have measured out my
life in coffee spoons."

—T. S. Eliot, "The Love Song of J. Alfred Prufrock"

A few choice accessories can make all the difference when you're brewing at home. To live your best coffee-lover life, check out the following gear.

Essential Equipment

- **Grinder:** A quality grinder is the single best investment you can make to elevate your coffee game. Look for burr grinders, which grind beans more consistently than blade grinders; they are available in both electric and manual models (the latter tend to be more affordable).

- **Scale:** Just like professional bakers, who are all about precision and accuracy, coffee lovers can benefit from a simple kitchen scale. Coffee beans vary in mass according to their roasting style, so it's recommended to measure them by weight, not volume. Choose a model that can be zeroed out (also known as the tare function); can measure to 1–2 decimal places; and can hold at least 4.5 pounds (2 kg), since most manual brewing devices sit on the scale throughout brewing.

- **Kettle:** While your trusty teakettle (both stovetop or electric) works just fine with devices such as the AeroPress and French press, pour-over methods call for a specialized model known as a gooseneck kettle, named after its long, curved spout. Gooseneck kettles are the key to achieving a more controlled and consistent pour.

Brewing Tools

- **Brewing device:** This depends on your personal preference. In the next chapter, we'll cover a variety of manual brewing methods, which might inspire you to try out a new device or hone your skills with one you already own.

- **Filters:** Unless you're brewing with a French press or Moka pot, you'll most likely need a good supply of filters on hand. Many devices require specially designed filters (although Melitta filters work well with several brands of pour-over cone drippers), so it's important to use the right filter for each brewing method.

- **Thermometer:** A thermometer can help ensure you're brewing with water that's within the right temperature range (195°F–205°F, or 90°C–96°C). Some stovetop gooseneck kettles feature a built-in thermometer; electric models also offer variable temperature controls.

- **Timer:** If your scale doesn't have a built-in timer, you can easily use your phone to keep track of brewing times. (Of course, there are smartphone apps such as KoHi and Brewseful to help with this, too.)

Serving and Storage

- **Brewing vessel and/or carafe:** Your chosen brewing method will determine whether or not you need additional tools for serving coffee. The Chemex and vacuum pot function as both brewing device and vessel; French press coffee should be poured immediately after brewing into a mug or a carafe, if you've brewed multiple servings.

- **Milk frother:** Handy for heating milk and whipping up cappuccinos and lattes (see page 79 for how to froth milk with a French press).

- **Storage containers:** Coffee can be stored in its original packaging or in opaque, airtight canisters made of ceramic or stainless steel. Look for options that have one-way degassing valves, which release carbon dioxide and keep your coffee fresh for longer.

POPULAR
ESPRESSO DRINKS

*"Espresso is a miracle of
chemistry in a cup."*

—**Andrea Illy**, 20th-century Italian coffee entrepreneur

Although coffee was discovered in Ethiopia, it was Italy that gave the coffee industry one of its most important innovations: espresso. What started out as a simple need for a faster cup of joe has since transformed the way coffee is consumed around the world.

A Brief History of Espresso

It all started in northern Italy at the turn of the twentieth century. The Industrial Revolution was in full swing, and factory owners noticed how coffee breaks helped fuel productivity. There was just one problem: filtered coffee took five minutes to brew, which they felt was much too long. This need for speed was at the heart of espresso's creation. The inventor Angelo Moriondo developed the world's first espresso machine in Turin in 1884, but the credit often goes to Luigi Bezzera, a Milanese manufacturer, who received a patent for improvements on Moriondo's design in 1901. It looked vastly different from today's espresso machines, but much of the process was the same.

The Italian word *espresso* literally means "pressed out." Espresso machines heat water until it's almost boiling and then use extreme pressure (unachievable by standard coffee makers) to force the water through finely ground coffee beans. The result is a cup brewed in a matter of seconds, not minutes. As the journalist Jimmy Stamp wrote in a 2012 article for *Smithsonian* magazine, espresso "could arguably be considered the first instant coffee."

The Four Ms

Espresso may be the name of a particular drink, but it is first and foremost a method of preparing coffee. These four elements are the pillars of espresso.

Miscela: Italian for "blend," the first pillar refers to using quality, freshly roasted coffee.

Macinazione: The second pillar is named after the Italian word for "grinding." Coffee should always be ground right before it's brewed—and for espresso, to a fine and uniform size.

Macchina: This pillar is all about the mighty espresso machine, which keeps water heated consistently and creates sufficient pressure to pull a shot.

Mano: Finally, the Italian word for "hand" refers to the role of the barista, whose manual skills and maintenance of the espresso machine influence the quality of the beverage.

Popular Espresso Drinks

When Howard Schultz (of Starbucks fame) visited Italy in 1983, he marveled at the "great theater" of espresso bars in Milan and enjoyed his first *caffè latte* in Verona. Thanks to his vision to re-create Italian coffee culture in the U.S. and beyond, cafés have never been the same.

And lattes are just the beginning. There's a whole spectrum of drinks made with a shot of espresso, from cortados to cappuccinos. It can be a little confusing to navigate a coffeehouse menu, so let's explore the range of espresso drinks. We'll look at each drink's strength and size and, if it's made with milk, the proportion of coffee to milk. In the next chapter, we'll cover how to make a few of these drinks at home.

Espresso

By definition, an espresso is 1 fluid ounce (30 ml) of highly concentrated coffee. It takes only 25 to 30 seconds to pull a shot of espresso, and it's served in a demitasse cup that holds around 2 to 3 ounces (60–90 ml). But don't be fooled by its small size: espresso packs a punch, offering intense flavors, lots of body, and that famous layer of crema (see Tip, opposite). Espresso is the base of all the drinks that follow, so we need a good espresso to have a good drink.

Tip: Beyond an espresso's diminutive size and daring flavors, one of its defining trademarks is the crema. Italian for "cream," it's the caramel-colored layer of foam on top of an espresso. Crema tells us two things: how much the beans were roasted (the darker the crema, the darker the roast), and how fresh the beans are. Fresh beans are full of oils and carbon dioxide that are released as coffee is brewed, regardless of the brewing method. With the added pressure of an espresso machine, these oils and gasses form tons of tiny bubbles, which ultimately make up the crema. The more bubbles, the fresher the beans.

Ristretto

A *ristretto* is espresso's little sibling—the process starts off the same, but the extraction is cut short by several seconds (the word means "restricted" in Italian). The final drink is about 15 to 20 milliliters, and because of the shorter extraction time, a ristretto is much sweeter and more acidic.

Lungo

The opposite of a *ristretto* is the *lungo* ("long" in Italian). A ristretto uses less hot water than an espresso, whereas a lungo uses nearly twice as much—typically around 50 milliliters. It also has a longer extraction time (up to a minute), resulting in a drink that has much more caffeine and bitterness.

Americano

A popular origin story of the *caffè Americano* (literally "American coffee") dates back to World War II, when U.S. troops were stationed in Italy. Unaccustomed to the intensity of espresso (not to mention the smaller serving size), American GIs wanted a taste of home, that is, drip coffee. So baristas began diluting espresso with hot water in larger cups. Today, an americano is prepared by pouring a double shot of espresso over hot water—that way, the crema stays intact.

Long Black

Developed in Australia and New Zealand, the long black is similar to an americano. Both involve pouring an espresso over hot water—the only difference is that less water is used for a long black, so the taste is not as diluted as an americano's.

Macchiato

A traditional macchiato—also known as espresso macchiato—is served in the same small demitasse cup as an espresso. It means "marked" in Italian, which provides a clue to its origin. In early-twentieth-century Italy, waiters couldn't always tell the difference

ESPRESSO DRINKS

Espresso

Ristretto

Lungo

Americano

Long Black

Macchiato

Cortado

Latte

Cappuccino

Flat White

Mocha

Red Eye

between a straight espresso and an espresso with a bit of steamed milk in it, so baristas would mark the latter with a dollop of foam.

Cortado

Most espresso drinks got their start in Italy, but not the cortado, which was invented in Spain. Its name means "cut" and refers to how a greater amount of milk cuts into an espresso's intense acidity. A cortado is equal parts espresso and steamed milk—not foam—and is typically served in a 4.5-ounce (130 ml) glass instead of a ceramic cup.

Latte

Latte is Italian for "milk," so it's little surprise that this drink features the greatest amount of milk in the largest cup (7–9 ounces, or 200–270 ml), giving it a milder, creamier taste compared to other espresso drinks. You won't often find lattes on an Italian café menu—they're usually prepared at home with a Moka pot (see page 87) and only for breakfast. In the rest of the world, a latte calls for a shot or two of espresso, followed by steamed milk, a thin layer of foamed milk, and beautifully executed latte art, of course.

Cappuccino

Like many other espresso drinks, the term *cappuccino* comes from Italy, only it isn't from the coffee world.

The Capuchin friars were an order of sixteenth-century monks whose light brown robes were remarkably similar to a cappuccino's color. Cappuccinos are made with equal parts espresso, steamed milk, and foamed milk—with a much more substantial layer of stiff foam than a latte. Because they're served in a smaller cup (around 6 ounces, or 180 ml) than lattes, cappuccinos offer a stronger flavor.

Flat White

Like the long black, the flat white is another espresso drink invented Down Under—Australia and New Zealand like to argue about who created it first—sometime in the 1980s. Rivalry aside, this drink is a happy medium between a latte and cappuccino. It's smaller and stronger than the former but is made with microfoam that creates a more velvety texture than the latter.

Mocha

All of the espresso drinks we've explored so far have involved two ingredients: coffee and milk. Mochas, also known as a *caffè mocha* or mocaccino, add a delectable new element to the mix. The addition of cocoa powder or chocolate syrup to a latte or cappuccino creates a sweet, creamy drink—essentially caffeinated hot chocolate.

Red Eye

Also known as a "shot in the dark," this drink is made by pouring a shot of espresso into a cup of regular drip or filtered coffee—perfect for those who need a serious caffeine boost. Drip coffee with a double shot of espresso is known as a "black eye."

BREWING
METHODS

MANUAL BREWING 101

*"Won't you have some coffee
before you go?"*

—Ludwig van Beethoven, *Memories of Beethoven*

Over the past twenty years, one of the greatest hallmarks of the third wave of coffee has been a renewed focus on manual brewing. Learning how to prepare better coffee at home not only helps coffee lovers highlight the unique aromas and flavors of each origin, but also honors the work of everyone who was a part of making our cup of specialty coffee possible. In this chapter, we'll learn the ins and outs of several key brewing methods, but first, let's get to know the main variables that will always be at play in making coffee, no matter which method we choose.

Brew Variables

As coffee lovers and home baristas, there are four main variables within our control:

1. GRIND SIZE
2. EXTRACTION TIME
3. WATER TEMPERATURE
4. COFFEE-TO-WATER RATIO

The goal isn't only to understand how each variable affects our coffee's taste; we also want to understand how these factors interact with one another so that we can properly adjust them. Just like a chef, we're not merely following a recipe—we have to know the purpose of every ingredient. The more familiar we are with each variable, the more flavors we can enjoy in our favorite beverage.

Grind Size

Choosing the right grind size is all about one thing: how much surface area of the coffee beans will the water be in contact with? The more finely ground the coffee is, the more contact it will have with water—and the more flavor compounds will be extracted from the beans.

Grind sizes have different levels, from extra fine and fine (often likened to granulated sugar) to medium and coarse (which looks and feels like kosher salt). When using a faster extraction method, such as an AeroPress (see page 80), the water and coffee have less contact time, so you'll want to use a finer grind size; the greater amount of surface area will compensate for the shorter extraction time. By contrast, brewing methods that take longer—such as a French

GRIND SIZE

Coarse

French press, cold
brew, coffee cupping

Medium-Coarse

Pour-over

Medium

Drip machine,
vacuum pot

Fine

Moka pot, AeroPress

Extra Fine

Turkish coffee

press—call for a coarser grind, because the coffee grinds and water will have more time to interact.

Extraction Time

Extraction is a fancy word for what happens when water interacts with all those fragrant, freshly ground coffee beans. Each bean is loaded with soluble compounds that dissolve in water and help give coffee its incredible aroma and flavors—especially the acidic, sweet, and bitter notes we love. However, it's important to know that these solubles don't dissolve at the same time. Acids are the first thing to be extracted, followed by sugars, and finally bitter notes, which take the longest time to dissolve in water.

The variable of time, then, is all about another brewing question: how many solubles are we extracting? If we keep the order of extraction in mind—acid, sweet, bitter—we can better understand the resulting flavors in our cup. If our coffee tastes sour, sharp, or overly acidic, we probably underextracted and should try a longer brew so that sweet and bitter notes have time to dissolve and round out the acidity. If our coffee tastes too bitter, even dull, it was most likely overextracted, and we should shorten the brewing time to compensate.

Water Temperature

This variable is all about speed—how fast is our extraction happening? The hotter the water, the faster all those soluble compounds will dissolve. Heat accelerates the extraction, so if we hold all the other variables constant, an increase in water temperature will extract more coffee in the same amount of time.

That said, we don't want to use water that's *too* hot. Boiling water often results in overextraction, which produces noticeable bitter and burnt notes. Likewise, water that isn't hot enough is unable to extract the full range of flavors, so we could end up with weak, underextracted coffee. Water's sweet spot is 195°F–205°F (90°C–96°C). Although you could use a thermometer to be precise, you can also try letting water come to a boil in your kettle and then give it a moment to cool before brewing.

Coffee-to-Water Ratio

When Beethoven wasn't composing symphonies or sonatas, he was avidly drinking coffee—and he was an early champion for this most important brewing variable. It is said that every morning, he would meticulously count out sixty coffee beans, which he believed was the perfect number for one cup of coffee.

Today, there's an easier way to figure out the right amount of coffee to brew with. The ideal ratio for manual brewing—which results in coffee with rich, well-balanced flavors—is between 1:15 and 1:18. The first number refers to a single gram of coffee beans; the second number tells us how many grams of water to use per gram of coffee.

> **Tip:** Because coffee beans aren't uniform in size and can vary by roasting style, it isn't recommended to measure them by volume (aka Beethoven's way). Instead, measuring coffee by weight helps us achieve more consistent results, no matter how the beans were roasted. Using the metric system also means we can calculate the amounts of both coffee and water with a single unit of measurement—which keeps things simple for our early-morning precoffee brains.

This variable is all about strength. The higher the second number in the ratio, the more water will be used in relation to coffee beans, producing a less concentrated brew. So let's say we want to make an 8-ounce mug of coffee. One fluid ounce is about 30 grams, so we should use 240 grams of water. Next, we divide the amount of water by the second number in the brew ratio we're using. For example, if we're brewing with a ratio of 1:16, we would divide 240 by 16;

that tells us to use 15 grams of coffee beans.

Are you confused yet? Fear not! This might feel a little complicated at first, but once you've found a good brew ratio for a particular brewing method, you can simply write down the amounts of coffee and water and refer back to them.

Key Brewing Steps

The five brewing devices covered in this chapter all look and function in very different ways, but their methods have a lot in common. Whether you're brewing with a V60 or vacuum pot, be sure to perform the following steps.

Grind in the moment. As we learned about on page 32, it's essential to grind coffee beans right before brewing to maximize their freshness and flavor.

Rinse your filter. This step is crucial if your brewing device uses a paper filter, such as an AeroPress and most pour-over methods. You should always rinse your filter with hot water and discard the rinse water before brewing so that any papery smell or filter taste won't make it into your beautiful cup of specialty coffee.

Preheat your vessel. In addition to your paper filter, rinse your brewing vessel with hot water (even if using a French press) and then discard it before brewing. This step helps warm your brewing vessel and ensures that less heat is lost once you pour hot water and start brewing.

Use a scale. Unless you're brewing with a Moka pot or vacuum pot, both of which need a heat source, most manual brewing devices will sit directly on the scale throughout brewing. This allows you to weigh coffee beans before grinding them and, just as important, to weigh your water while brewing (as measuring water before boiling it doesn't account for what will be lost to evaporation, throwing off your coffee-to-water ratio). After placing your device on the scale, add the ground coffee, zero out the scale (also known as the tare function), and then add the water.

Do a "bloom." Freshly roasted coffee is full of carbon dioxide, so as soon as hot water hits it, all that gas is quickly released as bubbles, or what's known as the *bloom*. These bubbles are a good sign that your beans are fresh, but they can also keep water from reaching the grinds and extracting enough delicious solubles. So to help your coffee brew as efficiently as possible, start with a bloom: pour a little water over the coffee (about 2–3 times the grams of coffee used) and then wait 30–45 seconds until bubbles stop forming.

Tip: For step-by-step brewing instructions, we recommend the websites of top roasters such as Stumptown and Blue Bottle Coffee, which offer in-depth visual guides for many popular brewing methods.

The Goal of Brewing

From determining brew ratios to weighing out coffee beans, manual brewing can sometimes feel like a lot of work, but it's all in pursuit of one goal: replicability. When we get a result we love, we want to conjure up that same balance of flavors or intensity again and again. The beauty of the brewing methods in this chapter is that many are accessible and affordable, meaning that you don't need anything too unusual or expensive to enjoy incredible coffee without changing out of your pajamas.

Electric Drip Coffee Makers

If you're short on time, electric drip coffee makers are still a better option than capsule or pod machines. The Specialty Coffee Association website lists certified home brewers that offer the right water temperature and brewing times. The following tips can also elevate your drip coffee game.

Use good water. As discussed on page 54, make sure to use filtered water that has the right balance of minerals.

Choose good beans. Better beans always make better coffee, so even when making drip coffee, opt for fresh beans from a specialty roaster (remember that coffee stays fresh for 2–3 weeks after roasting).

Grind in the moment. We've said it before and we'll say it again—grinding your coffee beans right before brewing makes a world of difference, and the same goes for a drip coffee maker.

Rinse your filter. Just as with manual brewing methods, do a thorough rinse of your paper filter first to ensure it doesn't pass on any unwanted flavors to your cup.

FRENCH PRESS

Even if you're new to the world of specialty coffee, chances are you're familiar with the French press. Also known as the *cafetière* or press pot, it's one of the simplest and best-known methods for manual brewing. True to its name, the French press was first patented in France in 1852, but it's the Swiss-Italian inventor Faliero Bondanini's 1958 design that we still use today. It has two key components: a glass or plastic container, often called a beaker, and a lid that includes a built-in plunger and mesh metal filter.

Brewing specifics

- **Grind size:** Coarse
- **Brewing time:** Approx. 4 minutes
- **Water temperature:** 195°F–205°F (90°C–96°C)
- **Brew ratio:** 1:16

How it works: A French press's brewing method is known as full immersion because the coffee is immersed in water throughout the extraction. Most recipes call for a four-minute brewing time, so use a coarse grind size to avoid overextraction. Also, use a burr grinder to ensure your coffee beans are evenly ground. An uneven grind has smaller particles that can slip through the metal filter and make your coffee gritty.

Why to use it: The French press is perfect for someone just starting out with manual brewing. It's widely available, simple to use, and requires no fancy kettles or tools.

What flavors to expect: The filter of a French press plays a big role in how the coffee tastes. Unlike absorbent paper filters, a metal filter allows oils and fine sediments to pass through, which give French press coffee its signature full-bodied flavor.

> **Tip:** A French press does more than just brew a bold cup of coffee; it can also be used to froth milk. Simply heat milk on the stove or in the microwave, pour it into your French press, and then rapidly plunge the filter up and down for 10–15 seconds until the milk begins to froth. In the next entry, we'll look at using an AeroPress to make espresso at home; with a little textured milk from a French press, you can begin whipping up your own lattes, too.

AEROPRESS

You might not think Fris-bees and coffee have much in common, but a few years ago, the American inventor and engineer Alan Adler proved otherwise. After inventing the Aerobie—a plastic fly-ing ring that once held the Guinness World Record for the longest throw—in 2005, he then turned his command of aerodynamics to coffee. Adler's goal was twofold: he wanted to create a better way of brewing a single cup of coffee, and he also wanted to reduce the level of bitterness extracted. The result? An entirely new brewing method that looks and func-tions like no other.

Brewing specifics

- **Grind size:** Fine
- **Brewing time:** 1–1½ minutes
- **Water temperature:** 175°F–185°F (80°C–85°C)
- **Brew ratio:** 1:12

How it works: Like a giant, plastic syringe, the AeroPress is made up of three parts. A cylindrical brewing chamber is placed over your mug before brewing; there's also a plunger and a filter cap that attaches to the bottom of the device. When the plunger is pushed down the chamber, air becomes trapped inside, which then forces water through the coffee grounds.

Why to use it: The plunger adds a fifth variable—pressure—to the process, making the AeroPress one of the quickest brewing methods out there. It's also the most versatile since it leaves lots of room to play with other variables. Depending on grind size and brew ratio, you can attain results similar to a French press, cold brew, or espresso (see Tip, page 82). Although initially it was slow to catch on, this ability to experiment is why the AeroPress is now beloved by coffee enthusiasts across the globe. There's even a World AeroPress Championship that inspires ever-new ways of using this unique device.

What flavors to expect: Because the AeroPress has such a short brewing time, you can use a fine grind size without risking overly bitter notes. The paper filter will absorb oils and sediment, resulting in a cleaner cup than you get with a French press. For even more acidity, use 2–3 paper filters at a time, producing a flavor similar to a pour-over. If you prefer the full body of a French press, metal AeroPress filters are available too.

Tip: By adding the element of pressure to manual brewing, the AeroPress can create a decent shot of espresso—crema and all! To capture an espresso's rich, concentrated flavors, you'll need to play with a few variables. Start off with a fine grind size and high ratio of coffee to water (a good brew ratio is usually around 1:3). Using these variables with a pour-over device would take too long for the water to filter through, leading to an overextraction, but thanks to the pressure of an AeroPress, the brewing time can be reduced to 25 seconds—just like with a commercial espresso machine.

CHEMEX

Just as Alan Adler brought his knowledge of aerodynamics to the AeroPress, a German inventor named Peter Schlumbohm drew on his doctorate in chemistry to create another famed brewing method. In 1941, he invented the Chemex—an elegant hourglass-shaped vessel that serves as both brewing device and carafe. Within years, the Chemex was a pop culture icon. It has made cameos in *Friends* episodes and Ian Fleming's kitchen in *From Russia with Love*, and it's the only coffee maker in the permanent collection of the Museum of Modern Art.

Brewing specifics

- **Grind size:** Medium-coarse
- **Brewing time:** Approx. 4 minutes
- **Water temperature:** 195°F–205°F (90°C–96°C)
- **Brew ratio:** 1:14–1:16 (depending on desired strength)

How it works: With the Chemex, we transition from immersion and pressure-based brewing to pour-over methods. Pour-over is a manual drip method, with water being poured over coffee grounds in a filter. Gravity draws the water down through the bed of coffee and into the vessel below. Many pour-over methods involve a cone dripper that sits directly on your mug (see "Additional Pour-Over Devices," page 86), but a Chemex's paper filter fits right into its upper funnel. It also features a distinctive wooden collar that allows the glass vessel to be held even when it contains hot coffee.

Why to use it: Beyond the cool appeal of its midcentury-modern design, the Chemex is all about technique, from ensuring the rinsed filter is properly arranged inside the funnel to pouring the water over the bed of coffee in slow, even circles. This works best with a gooseneck kettle, which gives you an incredible amount of control over the flow rate and accuracy of your pour. If you're a newcomer to manual brewing, the Chemex might seem a little complex, and it's not ideal if you're in a rush. Think of it as the perfect method for a leisurely Sunday morning.

What flavors to expect: Just as with a French press, the taste of Chemex coffee has everything to do with the filter. Chemex says its filters are 20% to 30%

thicker than other paper filters and catch nearly all oils and sediment. The result is a remarkably clean cup, which you can taste in its bright acidity and see in the brew itself. Simply hold up your Chemex to the light after brewing to see how shining and translucent the liquid is, taking on the color of honey. You'll also notice a lack of shimmering oils on your coffee's surface.

Additional Pour-Over Devices

Like many aspects of specialty coffee, pour-over is a world unto itself. The following cone drippers all sit directly on your mug and provide a clean cup that highlights each coffee's nuanced flavors and acidity.

The original pour-over: The paper coffee filter was invented in 1908 by a German housewife named Melitta Bentz, who was fed up with her percolator and the grounds that always ended up in her cup. Her prototype used a brass can and a filter made of blotting paper from her son's schoolbook. Gradually, it evolved into the design still used today: a plastic cone dripper that holds a paper filter and ground coffee. It's an affordable and accessible entry point into the world of pour-over.

Japanese innovations: Given Japan's famed coffee culture, it's little surprise that many top pour-over designs originated there. Check out the Kalita Wave, which has a distinctive flat bottom that helps control water flow; the Bee House, a ceramic cone dripper that can conveniently be used with Melitta filters; and the Hario V60, named after the 60-degree angle of its cone.

Pour-over meets full immersion: Created by the Taiwanese company Abid, the Clever Coffee Dripper looks like a standard pour-over device, but it differs in one key way: its design features a stopper mechanism, which doesn't let water pass through the filter until you release it. By combining the hands-off approach of a French press with the clean, filtered taste of pour-over coffee, it offers the best of both methods.

MOKA POT

The invention of espresso marked a huge milestone in how coffee was consumed around the world (see page 58). Yet the sheer size and cost of espresso machines meant that coffee in Italy was still most often enjoyed in public cafés and coffee bars into the early twentieth century. That all changed in 1933 with the invention of the Moka pot by the Italian engineer Alfonso Bialetti. Suddenly, espresso-style coffee could be made at home! Today, the device can be found in nine out of ten kitchens in Italy, not to mention in *Guinness World Records* as the world's most popular coffee maker.

Brewing specifics

- **Grind size:** Fine (almost as fine as you would use for espresso)
- **Brewing time:** Brewing is finished when you hear a bubbling or hissing sound.
- **Water temperature:** 212°F (100°C)
- **Brew ratio:** Approx. 1:7

How it works: Like the Chemex, the Moka pot's art deco design is iconic. The eight-sided aluminum device has three parts: a lower water chamber, a filter basket that holds the coffee grounds, and an upper chamber. Although electric models exist, traditional Moka pots are brewed on the stovetop, and they harness the same power of an espresso machine: steam pressure. As water heats in the bottom chamber, steam is created, which eventually generates enough pressure to force the water up through the ground coffee and into the top chamber.

Why to use it: Given the Moka pot's design and process, there are far fewer variables to control. The brew ratio will be determined by your device's filter basket and water chamber; you also can't control water temperature or brewing time. This makes it hard to avoid burning the coffee and extracting unwanted bitterness, which has made this brewing device less popular in the specialty coffee world. But depending on the taste you look for in coffee, the Moka pot could just be the one for you.

What flavors to expect: Also known as the stovetop espresso maker, the Moka pot is prized by espresso lovers for producing coffee with rich body and intense flavors. Although it may not have the same strength as commercial espresso, Moka pot coffee is said to be

2–3 times stronger than drip coffee. There are two steps you can take to reduce bitterness: fill the Moka pot with boiling water so that it doesn't need to be heated for as long on the stove, and after brewing, pour cold water over the lower chamber to cool the pot and halt extraction.

VACUUM POT

From the Chemex to the AeroPress, the history of coffee devices is dominated by male inventors and engineers. But in the 1840s in Lyon, France, a woman helped develop one of the most striking brewing methods. Her name was Marie Fanny Amelne Massot, but she filed for her patent under the nom de plume of Mme. Vassieux. She was not the first to invent the vacuum pot—also known as the vac pot or siphon coffee maker—nor its singular method of using vapor pressure to brew coffee, but the improvements she made on the existing design are markedly similar to the device still in use today.

Brewing specifics

- **Grind size:** Medium-coarse
- **Brewing time:** 2–2½ minutes
- **Water temperature:** 202°F (94°C)
- **Brew ratio:** Approx. 1:14

How it works: Just as in Mme. Vassieux's design, today's vacuum pots have two glass globes held in place by a metal frame. When a heat source is placed beneath the lower chamber (or bulb), water is heated, which gradually creates pressure and pushes the water up through a stem into the upper chamber (or hopper). Ground coffee is then added to the water and is allowed to brew for around 1½ minutes. Finally, the heat source is removed; this creates a vacuum in the lower bulb that draws the brewed coffee back down, leaving the grounds trapped by a filter up top.

Why to use it: With the presence of a heat source and steam pressure, the vacuum pot works a lot like a Moka pot, but thanks to its glass bulbs, we get to watch this fascinating process as it's happening. That is perhaps the biggest draw of this brewing method—it elevates a simple cup of coffee into a show. The vacuum pot may be fragile, costly, and a little too complex for everyday use, but from its inception it has been meant for putting coffee on display. Like a Japanese tea ceremony, the vacuum pot is perfect for slowing down and sharing a special beverage with guests.

What flavors to expect: The vacuum pot is a hybrid of brewing methods, bringing together elements of full immersion (when the coffee grounds and water are in contact in the upper chamber) and filtered coffee (when the brewed coffee passes through a metal, cloth, or paper filter on its way back down into the lower chamber). This combination is reflected in the flavors of a vacuum pot brew—it has the full body of French press coffee, plus the clean taste and lack of sediment achieved with pour-over devices such as the V60.

COLD BREW

"Iced Coffee. This . . . delicious
summer drink . . . is particularly
grateful on a wilting hot day."

—Ida C. Bailey Allen, 20th-century cookbook author
known as "The Nation's Homemaker"

Cold brew may feel like the latest trend in coffeeshops, but brewing coffee with cold water is one of the oldest ways of making the beverage. In fact, it predates all the other brewing methods in this chapter. In the 1600s, the Japanese were already cold-brewing tea when Dutch traders introduced them to coffee. But it wasn't until much later that the method gained broader recognition. In 1964 an American engineer named Todd Simpson tasted cold-brew coffee for the first time in Peru. Back in the U.S., he invented a cold-brew device that he christened the Toddy, which finally helped cement cold coffee's popularity.

Brewing specifics

- **Grind size:** Coarse
- **Brewing time:** 12–24 hours
- **Water temperature:** Cold or room temperature
- **Brew ratio:** 1:4–1:5 for cold-brew concentrate

How it works: The point of brewing coffee with hot water is that it speeds up the extraction process. Cold or room-temperature water drastically slows down brewing, which means we need to adjust the other variables substantially to achieve the right balance of flavors. We want to use a much greater proportion of coffee to water—usually 1:4 or 1:5 for cold-brew concentrate—and we're also going to prolong the extraction time, from a mere couple of minutes to as long as 24 hours. Here's an overview of the three main methods for brewing cold coffee.

- **Cold brew:** The simplest method can be made right in a Mason jar or French press, which should give you a clue to its brewing style—immersion. Just combine coarsely ground coffee and water, place the jar or French press in your fridge, and let it steep for 12–24 hours. After filtering the concentrate, you can then dilute it with water or milk.

Tip: Every time you open your fridge, give the jar or French press a little shake. This will mix up the coffee grounds and water and ensure a balanced extraction.

- **Cold drip:** Also known as Kyoto-style cold brew, this method is not as easy to try at home, but its impressive tower of containers makes for quite a show. The top chamber holds ice water and typically releases one drop per second into the middle chamber, which contains the coffee grounds. Each drop slowly makes its way through the coffee before being filtered into the bottom container. Cold drip is a slightly shorter process, taking between 3 and 12 hours.

- **Flash chill:** Many people feel that brewing coffee with cold water doesn't extract as many complex flavors and aromas, so the flash chill method— also called Japanese iced coffee—can help correct that. In this method, you brew coffee with hot water directly over ice, using a pour-over device such as the Chemex or V60. Another benefit: it's much faster than cold brew.

Why to use it: Yes, freshness is everything when it comes to hot coffee, but cold brew is much more shelf stable. Cold-brew concentrate can keep in your fridge for up to two weeks, though you might notice a drop in flavor after a week or so. It's also not as essential to use freshly roasted coffee for this method (although it certainly always helps), so if you've got some slightly older beans lying around, use them here. Cold brew is less acidic, so it's gentler on sensitive stomachs.

What flavors to expect: Cold brew offers a completely different flavor profile than hot coffee. Many of the compounds responsible for acidity and bitterness aren't soluble at low temperatures, unlike those that give coffee its sweet notes. Cold brew is thus naturally sweeter, but given the lower acidity, its smooth flavors are also less complex. Another important distinction: because cold-brew concentrate is prepared with a higher brew ratio, it will pack a stronger caffeine punch, so be sure to dilute the concentrate with 1–2 parts water or milk.

COFFEE TRADITIONS ACROSS THE WORLD

ETHIOPIAN
BUNA CEREMONY

~~~

"Buna dabo naw—*coffee is our bread.*"

—Ethiopian proverb

Ethiopia is not only the birthplace of coffee, it's also home to a centuries-old coffee ceremony imbued with rich symbolism and ritual. Named after the Amharic word for coffee, the ***buna* ceremony** is typically performed by a woman, who wears an embroidered white dress called a *habesha*. Before she begins, the hostess spreads flowers and grass across the floor as a symbol of abundance. She also burns incense—often frankincense or myrrh—to clear away bad spirits and passes around snacks such as popcorn and peanuts to guests. From the first moment, the Ethiopian coffee ceremony is a delight for the senses.

Because this ceremony calls for green coffee beans, the hostess must carry out several key steps, including washing the raw beans, roasting them on a flat pan over a charcoal stove, and walking the pan around the room so guests may enjoy the fragrance of the freshly roasted coffee. She then grinds the beans by hand using a wooden mortar and pestle before boiling them in a dark clay pot called the *jebena*. Its rounded shape and thin spout help filter the grounds as the coffee is served into small handleless cups called *cini*. Pouring the coffee is a serious art; the hostess will hold the jebena a foot high and serve the coffee in one continuous stream. After the first round, the grounds are brewed again. There are three rounds in all—the first and strongest brew is called *abol*; the second, *tona*; and the final brew, *baraka*. Even though it is the weakest brew, *baraka* means "to be blessed," for it is believed that guests are indeed blessed by the ceremony and that by the third round their spirits have been transformed.

The Ethiopian coffee ceremony isn't just for special occasions; it's often performed two or three times a day, as an important part of daily life and hospitality. Because it can take up to an hour for the first cup to be served, the ceremony is about much more than coffee. It's about connection—taking time to gather with loved ones, neighbors, or visitors and sharing the latest news, stories, and perhaps even a bit of gossip. In Ethiopia, one's community—just like coffee itself—is meant to be savored.

Notable destinations: For coffee lovers, there's no greater destination than Ethiopia. Besides experiencing its coffee ceremony and visiting estates such as Bebeka—the country's largest coffee farm—the real adventure is glimpsing coffee in the wild. About 300 miles southwest of Addis Ababa lies Kaffa, one of the oldest coffee-producing regions in the world. There, the UNESCO-protected Kafa Biosphere Reserve shelters acres of wild coffee forests, including some 5,000 varieties of arabica!

ARABIC
QAHWA

~~~

"No one can understand the truth until he drinks
of coffee's frothy goodness."

—Sheik Abd-al-Kadir, 12th-century founder
of the Qadiri order of Sufism

From the highlands of Ethiopia, coffee made its way across the Red Sea to Yemen. As it continued to spread throughout the Arabian Peninsula, so too did the tradition of Arabic coffee, or *qahwa,* develop. As with Ethiopian coffee rituals, there is a strong ceremonial element to making and serving Arabic coffee. It also uses green coffee beans, which are similarly roasted and ground using a copper mortar and pestle while guests look on.

Like Turkish coffee, which developed around the same time (page 104), Arabic coffee is boiled but not filtered before being served. However, there are several differences. It is often prepared with spices—especially cardamom, but also cloves, cinnamon, and saffron—which are either ground together with the beans or added to the coffee while it's boiling. Coffee is brewed in an elegant metal pitcher called the *dalla*, which features a long arching spout, and then served to guests in small decorative cups called *finjān*. Arabic coffee is traditionally consumed black and unsweetened. To counter the coffee's thick bitter taste and to add a bit of sweetness, it is often served with dates and other dried fruits.

In 2015, UNESCO declared Arabic coffee an intangible cultural heritage of Arab states, describing it as an "act of generosity" and hospitality. To this day, coffee is an important part of cultures across western Asia, from Saudi Arabia and Syria to Lebanon and Iraq. In Jordan, Arabic coffee is known as *qahwah sādah*—"welcome coffee." Historically, in Palestine, when a guest finished their final cup, it was customary to say to the host, "*Dyman.*" Arabic for "always," the word implied, "May you always have the means to serve coffee." In return, the host would answer, "*Sahteen,*" wishing their guest "good health."

Notable destinations: From a coffee museum in Dubai to a cultural coffee experience in Abu Dhabi called Bait Al Gahwa, there are countless ways to discover Arabic coffee. But the most compelling coffee destination in the region is sadly off-limits for now. For years, Yemen has been devastated by an ongoing civil war, but it is also home to some of the rarest coffee in the world, which grows on terraces built into the country's arid mountains.

SENEGAL'S
CAFÉ TOUBA

Named after the West African city in which it was created, *café Touba* is made by mixing coffee with cloves and a signature ingredient—a peppery spice known as grains of Selim, or *djar* in the Wolof language. Coffee beans and spices are roasted together, ground to a fine powder, and then brewed with a cloth filter. Café Touba is typically enjoyed black and aerated during serving by pouring the coffee back and forth between two containers, much like South Indian filter coffee (page 121).

This tradition dates to the turn of the twentieth century, when a Sufi saint named Cheikh Ahmadou Bamba, who founded the Mouride brotherhood and the holy city of Touba, developed café Touba to help his followers stay alert for all-night chanting sessions. The drink is now so popular throughout Senegal that, in 2010, Nestlé released an instant coffee called Nescafé Ginger & Spice to try to keep up with the competition.

Notable destinations: Though it originated in its namesake city, café Touba is now enjoyed all across Senegal. Roaming coffee vendors and street-side kiosks called *tangana* are a ubiquitous presence, especially in the country's capital of Dakar.

TURKEY'S
TÜRK KAHVESI

~~~

*"A single cup of coffee commits one to
forty years of friendship."*
—Turkish proverb

After Yemen, the next country that played a pivotal role in coffee's expansion was Turkey. By 1555, the first coffeehouse had been opened in Istanbul, and coffee became known as "the milk of chess players and thinkers."

But the greatest coffee legacy that Turkey gave the world was a preparation method still in use today. Turkish coffee, or *Türk kahvesi*, is brewed with extremely fine grounds, even finer than those used for espresso, and it's prepared in a special coffee pot called a *cezve*, which features a long handle and is traditionally made from brass or copper. The powdery grounds are mixed with cold water in the cezve and then heated on the stovetop until the coffee is foaming but has not yet boiled over. Sugar is added to the grounds before they're boiled, so if you take your coffee sweet, be sure to request your desired level of sweetness while ordering: from *sade* for unsweetened, to *orta şekerli* for medium sugar, to *şekerli* for maximum sweetness.

The strong unfiltered coffee is then poured into small decorative cups called *kahve fincanı* (which have handles and saucers, unlike Arabic coffee cups). It is always served with a glass of water to cleanse the palate, as well as a small sweet—such as *lokum*, or Turkish delight—to balance the bitterness. A final ritual is the Turkish tradition of *fal*, or having one's fortune read in the coffee grounds left in the cup.

Notable destinations: Istanbul has been home to coffeehouses for nearly 500 years, from Şark Kahvesi in the bustling Grand Bazaar to Mandabatmaz near Taksim Square (the name means "water buffalo doesn't sink," referring to just how thick Turkish coffee is). For traditional coffee souvenirs, stop by the Spice Bazaar.

AUSTRIA'S
WIENER MELANGE

"Where time and space are consumed,
but only the coffee is found on the bill."

—UNESCO Intangible Cultural Heritage
on Viennese Coffee House Culture

Since its discovery, coffee had always been served black, but that began to change in the seventeenth century—and it all started with a siege, a spy, and a swift retreat.

During the second Siege of Vienna in 1683, things were looking grim for the defending city. It had been surrounded by the Ottoman army and no help appeared on the horizon. But a certain Polish diplomat was living in Vienna at the time. His name was Georg Franz Kolschitzky, and he had a knack for languages, from Hungarian to Serbian to Turkish, which he'd picked up during his time in Istanbul. And so, in an act of heroism remembered to this day, Kolschitzky disguised himself as a Turkish soldier, walked right through the enemy's camp (it's said he even sang out Ottoman songs as he walked), and got a message to a nearby duke, requesting urgent backup. Help soon arrived and the Ottoman army was sent packing.

In their hasty retreat, the Turks left behind 500 sacks of green coffee beans, which many assumed to be camel food—but Kolschitzky knew exactly what they were, thanks again to his knowledge of and experience with Turkish customs. He used those beans to open one of Vienna's first cafés, the Blue Bottle. To make Turkish coffee more appealing to the European palate, he added milk. Kolschitzky is thus credited with inventing the *Wiener Melange*—a drink similar to a cappuccino, made with a shot or two of espresso and foamy steamed milk—and is considered a patron saint of coffeehouses even today.

Notable destinations: So renowned is the Austrian capital for its cafés that in 2011, UNESCO added Viennese coffeehouse culture to its list of intangible cultural heritage. Coffee lovers could easily spend a week lingering in these timeless gathering places of delicious drink and food. Savor a decadent slice of *sachertorte* at Café Sacher; watch pastry chefs at work in Café Demel; and enjoy live music performances at Café Schwarzenberg, the first coffeehouse built along the Ringstrasse in 1861.

FRANCE'S
CAFÉ AU LAIT

Just as the Turkish were responsible for coffee's arrival in Austria, an Ottoman ambassador is credited with popularizing the drink in France. In 1669, Suleiman Aga arrived in Paris, and among his entourage was a chief coffee maker. Quite the ladies' man, Aga loved to entertain and host coffee ceremonies. Although he lived in Paris for less than a year, he made such an impression on his high-society guests that coffee became firmly established in French culture from then on.

Around the time that the *Wiener Melange* was developed in Vienna, a similar drink evolved in Paris—*café au lait*, French for "coffee with milk." It is made by combining equal parts steamed milk and strong brewed coffee. Traditionally served in a bowl, café au lait is most often enjoyed at breakfast, where it goes beautifully with a warm and flaky croissant.

Notable destinations: For a taste of French coffee history, head to the elegant Café Procope in Paris's Latin Quarter. Founded in 1686, it is the oldest café in the city still in operation. Former patrons include Rousseau, Voltaire, and Napoleon.

SWEDISH
FIKA

~~~

Just as all the world's top coffee-producing countries can be found along the Bean Belt (see page 23), the countries that *consume* the most coffee are concentrated in one geographic region: Scandinavia. Given the long arctic winters and months of perpetual darkness, perhaps it's little surprise that Europe's northernmost countries have such a fondness for the cozy comfort of coffee. Beating out Denmark, Norway, and Iceland, Sweden has the second highest coffee consumption per capita. It's also home to the beloved coffee ritual known as *fika*.

Fika (pronounced "FEE-ka") literally means "to have coffee" and is said to be an inversion of the nineteenth-century Swedish word for coffee, *kaffi*. But the ritual of fika involves so much more than just a steaming cup of coffee (or tea). First of all, it is always accompanied by pastries, which are collectively known as *fikabröd*. Popular Swedish treats include cinnamon buns (*kanelbullar*), chocolate balls (*chokladbollar*), and cakes, as well as open-faced sandwiches known as *smorgas*.

In a way, fika has a lot in common with British afternoon tea, but a key difference is the frequency with which the two rituals are observed. Fika is nothing short of a social institution in Sweden. At least twice a day, whether you're at work or home, it's customary to slow down, gather with friends or colleagues for some coffee and pastries, and take a break (*fikapaus*) or rest (*fikarast*). Many Swedish companies even have a dedicated fika room. One 2013 study showed that, on average, Swedes spend 227 hours a year having fika—that's almost ten days!

Notable destinations: When you're searching for the perfect fika spot in Sweden, here's a couple words that might come in handy: *fik* is slang for café, and *konditori* refers to a coffeehouse or patisserie. One acclaimed café in Stockholm is Vete-Katten, which has been open since 1928. Its founder, Ester Nordhammar, had little experience with baking, but she was determined to hire only women—and with their help, she soon built a delicious pastry empire.

FINLAND'S
KAFFEOST

~~~~~~~

*"When the body is exhausted, a cup of
coffee is a true helper."*

—Finnish proverb

Finland consistently ranks as the top coffee consumer in the world. Finns consume an impressive 27 pounds (12 kg) of coffee beans per capita each year. And these beans are typically light-roasted and brewed in an electric drip coffee maker.

It's not unusual to drink 8–9 cups of coffee a day in Finland, so the Finns have developed special words to describe having coffee at a certain time or in a specific situation; these include *aamukahvi* (morning coffee), *iltakahvi* (evening coffee), and *saunakahvi* (sauna coffee). There's also *mitalikahvit*, which means "medal coffee" and refers to drinking coffee when a Finnish athlete or team wins a sports competition, and *vaalikahvit*, Finnish for "election coffee." As Yle News reported in 2019, having coffee and a sweet treat after voting "is seen as inseparable from the act of voting itself."

The medal for Finland's most surprising coffee tradition has to be awarded to *kaffeost*—coffee with cheese. The recipe doesn't call for any old kind of cheese—*leipäjuusto* must be used. Finnish for "bread cheese," it's known in the U.S. as Finnish squeaky cheese and has a similar texture to halloumi. Just as you might add marshmallows to hot chocolate, cubes of cheese are placed in a mug before hot black coffee is poured over them (like halloumi, the cheese softens but doesn't melt). Another option is to snack on slices of cheese as you drink coffee, along with generous servings of tangy cloudberry jam.

Notable destinations: Kaffeost originated in the far north of Scandinavia, especially in the communities of the indigenous Sámi people in Lapland. They traditionally prepared the drink in wooden mugs known as *guksi*, which were carved out of a single birch burl. The Swedish food creator Eva Gunnare often serves kaffeost on tours and home visits offered by her company, Essence of Lapland.

GERMANY'S
PHARISÄER

Germany holds a few coffee distinctions. It is the world's second-largest importer of coffee. In 1908, it was the German housewife Melitta Bentz in Dresden who invented the paper coffee filter (see page 86). And then there's the *Pharisäer*, a decadent German drink that combines strong coffee, a shot of rum, a bit of sugar, and whipped cream.

According to legend, the drink came about in the nineteenth century because of a North Frisian pastor named Gustav Beyer who was firmly opposed to alcohol. To enjoy a nip without the preacher knowing, villagers at a festival one year added rum to their coffee and covered it with whipped cream to mask the telltale scent. When Beyer noticed their trick, he is said to have exclaimed, "*Ihr Pharisäer!*" (You Pharisees!), and the name stuck.

Notable destinations: Not far from Melitta Bentz's hometown is Germany's oldest coffeehouse, Zum Arabischen Coffee Baum. Opened in 1711, the historic café is located in old town Leipzig and has a free coffee museum on site.

IRISH COFFEE

"Only Irish coffee provides in a single glass all four essential food groups: alcohol, caffeine, sugar, and fat."

—Alex Levine, 20th-century Irish actor and musician

During the 1940s, Ireland's rugged west coast was the final stop for planes making their way from Europe to North America. One stormy winter's night in 1943, a flight headed for New York was forced to turn around and return to Foynes Airport. There was a restaurant on site, led by head chef Joe Sheridan. When he heard about the returning plane, he concocted a special drink to warm up the tired passengers—adding a shot of whisky, brown sugar, and lightly whipped cream to strong brewed coffee. One traveler asked Sheridan if he'd used Brazilian coffee in the drink. The chef is said to have replied, "No, it was Irish coffee!" and the rest is history.

Notable destinations: Foynes Airport in western Ireland is now home to the Foynes Flying Boat & Maritime Museum, where coffee lovers can pay homage to Sheridan's creation in the Irish Coffee Lounge.

AMERICA'S COWBOY COFFEE

"The insatiable appetite acquired
by travellers upon the Prairies is
almost incredible, and the quantity
of coffee drank is still more so."
—**Josiah Gregg**, *Commerce of the Prairies*

Since the American Revolution, coffee has reigned supreme over tea in the U.S.—and that was perhaps never truer than during the westward expansion of the nineteenth century, when scores of settlers and pioneers aimed their wagons west. Coffee became their fuel. As the trader Josiah Gregg observed in 1844, "It is an unfailing and apparently indispensable beverage, served at every meal—even under the broiling noon-day sun, the wagoner will rarely fail to replenish a second time, his huge tin cup."

Cowboys especially lived on coffee, and they loved it hot, black, strong, and thick—thick enough, even, for a horseshoe to float on. As one wagon cook exhorted, "If the hoss shoe sinks, she ain't ready." Their signature brewing method became known as cowboy coffee, and it's made in a similar way to French press coffee but without a filter. The no-fuss method starts by boiling water in a pot over a campfire; coarsely ground coffee is then added and given time to steep. Because a "crust" of grounds forms on the surface, as with a French press, a little cold water is poured into the pot, which helps the grounds settle to the bottom. The final trick is pouring the coffee slowly enough so that most of the grounds stay in the pot.

Notable destinations: Cowboy coffee originated in the American West, but venture even farther west and you'll reach Hawaii, which is the only commercial coffee-producing region in the U.S. There are coffee plantations on five major Hawaiian islands, but the Kona region on the Big Island is especially noteworthy (see page 48). There, you can tour some of its 600 coffee farms, learn about coffee pioneers at the Kona Coffee Living History Farm, and attend the annual Kona Coffee Cultural Festival, held every November.

COLOMBIA'S
TINTO

"The coffee tradition is the most representative symbol of national culture in Colombia."

—UNESCO World Heritage List

Colombia is a coffee powerhouse. It's the world's third-largest producer (after Brazil and Vietnam) and is hailed for high-quality arabica beans and well-balanced flavors—but its renowned coffee industry almost didn't happen.

When the first coffee seeds were brought to the country by Jesuit missionaries in the sixteenth century, local farmers were less than enthusiastic to plant them. Coffee trees take around five years to bear their first crop, a bit long for growers to wait. But a village priest named Francisco Romero had an idea to help coffee catch on: when farmers came to him for confession, he would tell them to plant three or four coffee trees as their penance. After several years, this unorthodox atonement began to bear fruit. In 1835, the first 2,500 bags of Colombian coffee were exported to the U.S., and they haven't stopped since.

Today, the lower-quality beans that aren't good enough to be exported out of Colombia are used to make a beloved traditional drink known as *tinto*. Named after the Spanish word for "dark red," tinto is similarly dark and rich in color—in fact, it's most often served black. Tinto is available everywhere from homes to cafés to city streets, where it's sold by roving vendors. From Cartagena to Cali, tinto sellers are ubiquitous. They push carts or carry wooden trays laden with thermoses, and for just a few cents, anyone can enjoy a small Styrofoam cup of sweet, steaming coffee.

Notable destinations: Colombia boasts some 600,000 coffee growers across the country, but one region stands out. The *Zona Cafetera*, or Coffee Triangle, is home to countless coffee farms, not to mention the National Coffee Park, a theme park dedicated entirely to coffee. In 2011, UNESCO officially recognized this region as the Coffee Cultural Landscape of Colombia.

MEXICO'S
CAFÉ DE OLLA

This traditional spiced coffee from Mexico is named after the earthenware pot it's prepared in. ***Café de olla*** means "coffee from a pot" in Spanish, and the ceramic pot is said to impart flavor to the coffee itself, much like clay teapots do in the world of tea.

But that isn't the only parallel between the two drinks—like masala chai in India, café de olla is full of aromatic spices and flavors. Cinnamon is the most common spice added, followed by cloves, star anise, and orange peel; it's sweetened with an unrefined cane sugar known in Mexico as *piloncillo*. And just as spiced medicinal drinks had been prepared in India

for centuries before the British introduced tea to the country, café de olla predates the arrival of coffee in Mexico during the colonial era. Indeed, the practice of adding spices to hot drinks such as *pinole* and *atole* (both made from ground corn, cacao, and other spices) has been deeply rooted in indigenous Mexican communities since ancient times.

These traditional drinks were finally married with coffee during a pivotal moment in history: the Mexican Revolution, which took place from 1910 to 1920. Thousands of women took part in the war effort, helping set up camps and cook for soldiers. Many say that it was there that café de olla was born—in the giant clay pots in which the women prepared coffee every morning, helping to energize soldiers while drawing on the rituals of their past.

Notable destinations: Oaxaca City in southern Mexico is well-known as a foodie's paradise—and for coffee lovers, the surrounding foothills of the Sierra Madre de Oaxaca mountain range are also home to numerous coffee plantations and *fincas*. Founded in 1880, Finca Las Nieves is one of many farms that offer organic coffee tours, plus overnight stays in adobe cabins.

SOUTH INDIAN FILTER COFFEE

Around the world, India is famous for its sweet, spice-infused masala chai, but tea is very much a northern Indian tradition. In south India, a different hot drink has historically been preferred over chai: rich, creamy **filter coffee**. But the filter used for this tradition is unlike anything we've seen thus far. It's a slim stainless-steel cylinder, made of two parts—the upper half functions as the brewing chamber and is perforated at the bottom; the lower half is where the coffee is collected.

The brewing process for South Indian filter coffee is just as unique. Finely ground coffee is placed in the upper chamber and gently pressed down by a steel tamper, which comes with the filter and has small holes punched in it. Boiling water is then poured into the filter, a little at a time; it's important to wait until the water fully seeps through the grounds before adding more. This can take anywhere from 15 to 30 minutes, sometimes longer; the resulting coffee is so strong (stronger even than espresso), it's known as a decoction, which is a more concentrated version of an infusion that extracts the essence of a plant, root, or bark.

Only a tablespoon or two of this decoction is

used for each serving. The coffee is combined with sugar and boiled milk and then served in a small stainless-steel tumbler, which is set inside a deep saucer called the *dabarah*. Before drinking, the coffee is poured back and forth between the tumbler and saucer. This helps cool the drink and mix all the ingredients; most important, it aerates the coffee, giving it a sought-after layer of frothy bubbles on top.

Notable destinations: Follow in Baba Budan's footsteps (see page 43) and head to India's original coffee region—Baba Budangiri, in the southern state of Karnataka—where coffee farms and plantations abound.

INDONESIA'S
KOPI LUWAK

Since the Dutch began exporting coffee from the East Indies to Europe in 1711, Indonesia has been a top coffee producer—and the source of one of the world's most expensive coffees: *kopi luwak*. *Luwak* is another name for the Asian palm civet, a mammal the size of a cat. Nineteenth-century Dutch plantation owners didn't allow native workers to pick coffee for their own consumption; but locals discovered that civets would eat coffee cherries, and whole beans could be collected from (and cleaned of!) their excrement.

Over time, kopi luwak grew in fame, due in part to the claim that enzymes in the civet's digestive tract create a coffee that's smoother and less bitter. But coffee pros say that not only is kopi luwak low in quality and not deserving of its high price, it's also unethical. What started as a natural process in the wild now involves civets living in captivity, force-fed only coffee cherries.

Notable destinations: Avoid touristy kopi luwak tastings, and head to Indonesia's more authentic coffee-growing islands, such as Sumatra, Sulawesi, and Java. Ethical Indonesian coffee traditions include *kopi jahe*, which combines brewed coffee with piquant fresh ginger and palm sugar.

VIETNAM'S
CÀ PHÊ SỮA ĐÁ

Just as Jesuit priests brought coffee to Colombia and encouraged its growth across the country, so a French Catholic missionary is said to have carried a single coffee tree to Vietnam in 1857. Only a century and a half later, Vietnam is now the second-largest coffee producer in the world—but unlike Colombia's high-quality arabica, 97% of the coffee exported from Vietnam today is robusta. Vietnam is also home to a coffee tradition that transforms harsh robusta beans, which are notoriously bitter, into a rich, refreshing drink: *cà phê sữa đá*, which means "iced coffee with milk"—specifically, sweetened condensed milk.

As with many Vietnamese coffee drinks, cà phê sữa đá starts with a metal drip filter called the *phin*, which is small enough to sit on top of a glass. Medium- to coarsely ground coffee is placed in the filter, and hot water is poured over the grounds and then allowed to slowly filter through the coffee. Much like South Indian filter coffee (see page 121), the result is a highly concentrated brew, which is then combined with ice and condensed milk. Alternately, the coffee concentrate can be consumed hot and black (*cà phê nóng*), black over ice (*cà phê đá*), or hot with condensed milk (*cà phê sữa nóng*).

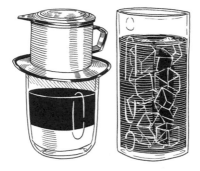

Notable destinations: From Hanoi to Ho Chi Minh City, Vietnam has a thriving café culture, but its ultimate "capital of coffee" is the growing region of Buon Ma Thuot, located in Dak Lak province in the country's Central Highlands. In addition to visiting its many coffee plantations, you can also attend a biennial coffee festival held every other March and explore the Trung Nguyen Coffee Village, an open-air museum spread across nearly 50,000 acres.

THAILAND'S
OLIANG

~~~

Another popular coffee tradition in Southeast Asia is Thai iced coffee—or *oliang*, from the Thai Chinese words for "black" (*o*) and "cold" (*liang*). Oliang looks a lot like Vietnamese iced coffee, but the two drinks differ in a few ways. For starters, the coffee used to make oliang features several ingredients besides coffee. Brands such as Pantai include corn, cardamom, sesame seeds, soybeans, and rice, and it's commonly sold as a powdered blend.

Thai iced coffee is also prepared differently. Instead of a metal drip filter, the coffee blend is placed into a cloth bag that's attached to a wireframe ring and handle. This filter is known as a *tungdtom* in Thailand, but given its long unique shape, it's often referred to as a "coffee sock" across the world. True to its name, oliang is served black over ice or with condensed milk.

Notable destinations: Coffee farms thrive in Thailand's northern highlands. The coffee village of Doi Chang is an easy day-trip from Chiang Rai, where you can visit numerous plantations and processing facilities.

JAPAN'S
KAN KŌHĪ

〜〜〜

*"My mission is to pass on the magic of coffee
to as many people as possible."*

—**Tadao Ueshima,** founder of
Ueshima Coffee Company

Vending machines are everywhere in Japan (fun fact: the country has one vending machine for every 23 people!), and one of the most common items they're stocked with is another Japanese icon—canned coffee, or as it's better known in Japan, **kan kōhī**. The first commercial canned coffee was launched in 1969 by the Ueshima Coffee Company (UCC), whose founder, Tadao Ueshima, wanted to transform coffee into "a drink to be enjoyed anytime, anywhere." Today, the variety of canned coffee is dizzying. Dozens of brands—including Boss, Georgia, Nescafé, and Fire—offer canned coffee in nearly every available style: milky or black, sweetened or unsweetened, and, perhaps most impressive, hot and cold options.

Notable destinations: The city of Kobe is home to UCC headquarters and Japan's only coffee museum, which was opened in 1987 on International Coffee Day (October 1). It includes exhibits covering all six steps in how coffee is made, as well as a tasting corner with daily themed events. The museum's modern exterior is designed after a mosque to honor coffee's deep roots with Sufi mystics.

SERVING
COFFEE

HOW TO HOST A COFFEE CUPPING

Cupping is a process for tasting coffee that is used by growers, buyers, and roasters, particularly to score specialty coffee. But you don't have to be an industry professional to host your own version. For beginners and experts alike, cupping is an excellent way to enjoy multiple coffees at once and to discover the unique flavors of each one. Here's the rundown on how to cup coffee like a pro.

Supplies needed:

- Whole coffee beans
- Coffee grinder
- Kitchen scale
- Timer
- Kettle
- Filtered water
- Cold sparkling water
- Cupping vessels or bowls
- Soup spoons
- Glass of hot water for rinsing spoons
- Bowl for used coffee grounds
- Notebook or cupping form (optional)

1. Select your coffees. Decide on 3–4 single-origin coffees from a variety of growing regions; for instance, one coffee each from Latin America, Africa, and Asia.

2. Set up your supplies. For your cupping vessels, use identical glass or white porcelain cups or small bowls that hold around 6–8 fluid ounces (180–240 ml). Set out 2 cups per coffee so that you can brew and sample coffees all at once (brewing 2 cups of each will help ensure consistent flavors and aromas). Place a soup spoon at each setting for the tasters.

3. Grind the beans. As always, grind your beans in the moment to maximize freshness and flavor. Start by grinding a few extra grams and discarding them; this will purge your grinder of the previous variety, allowing you to better taste each sample. Then grind the amount needed for tasting. Coffee cuppings call for a medium-coarse grind, and *The Blue Bottle Craft of Coffee* handbook suggests a brew ratio of 1:17 (for more about grind sizes and brew ratios, see "Manual Brewing 101" on page 68).

> **Tip:** A common misconception is that uncooked rice grains can be used to clean your coffee grinder. Top grinder companies advise against it, and Baratza even refuses to repair products that have been damaged this way.

4. Smell the dry aroma. Before brewing, take a moment to appreciate the fragrance of each dry, freshly ground coffee. Ask yourself what you're noticing and sensing; you can even write down your observations in a notebook or on an official cupping form.

5. Brew. One of the main points of the cupping process is to taste each coffee in its purest form, without any intervention from a filter. And you don't need fancy brewing devices, either. Once you've placed the ground coffee in each cup, simply pour filtered water (heated to 205°F, or 96°C) over the grounds and let them steep for 4 minutes.

6. Break the crust and smell the wet aroma. Just as with other full immersion methods, such as the French press, a crust of coffee grounds will form on top. Before you break the crust with your spoon, be sure to lean in close so you're ready to breathe in the pungent wet aroma as it escapes. Pay special attention to how it differs from the dry aroma.

7. Remove the grounds. Use two spoons to skim as many grounds as possible off the surface of each cup. Place the used grounds in a separate bowl, and have a glass of hot water on hand for rinsing your spoon between each coffee.

8. Taste the coffee—and don't forget to slurp! Slurping may be frowned upon in many social situations, but at the cupping table, hearty slurps are encouraged. It helps generate a little spray in your mouth, so you can better taste all the flavors on your palate.

9. Describe each coffee. After all that smelling and slurping, this step is what coffee tastings are ultimately about. Describing a coffee's acidity or body is important, but also try to name its unique flavor notes—and make connections between what you're tasting and any memories or past experiences you're reminded of.

> **Tip:** The ability to name flavors is very much a skill, so it might be helpful to use a resource called the Coffee Taster's Flavor Wheel (see page 134 for more).

10. Rinse and repeat. Coffee's taste changes as it cools, so cycle back through your coffees multiple times to observe how they evolve over time. Don't forget to keep rinsing your spoon, and sip sparkling water between each coffee to cleanse your palate.

Coffee Flavor Evaluation

Developed by the Specialty Coffee Association in 1995 and updated in 2016 in collaboration with World Coffee Research, the Coffee Taster's Flavor Wheel features 110 attributes for describing a coffee's aroma and taste. This resource is used by coffee industry professionals and can help us coffee lovers hone our ability to describe a coffee's aroma and taste. Here are just a few descriptors included on the wheel.

Fruity

Berry: blackberry, raspberry, strawberry

Citrus: grapefruit, orange, lemon, lime

Dried: raisin, prune

Sweet

Brown sugar: honey, caramelized, maple syrup

Cocoa: chocolate, dark chocolate

Other

Floral: chamomile, rose, jasmine

Spices: clove, cinnamon, nutmeg, anise, pepper

Nutty: almond, hazelnut, peanuts

COFFEE COCKTAILS

From Irish coffee to Germany's *Pharisäer* (see pages 114 and 113), coffee and alcohol have long been a winning combination. Channel your inner barista *and* bartender and give these coffee cocktails a try.

Classic: You can never go wrong with an ice-cold espresso martini, which combines freshly brewed espresso with vodka and coffee liqueur (add the hot espresso to your shaker last so it won't have time to melt the ice). *Calls for 1 fluid ounce of espresso.*

Cool: Cold-brew concentrate (see page 93) makes an excellent addition to many of your favorite cocktails. Try out a cold-brew gin and tonic for a refreshing lift. *Calls for 1½ fluid ounces of cold-brew concentrate.*

Campari: Did someone say *aperitivo*? Cold brew is a natural fit with timeless Italian cocktails such as the Americano and Negroni. *Calls for 1–1½ fluid ounces of cold-brew concentrate.*

Cozy: For a decadent French connection coffee, add Cognac and amaretto to hot filter coffee and top with whipped cream and shaved almonds. *Calls for 6 fluid ounces of black coffee.*

COFFEE TRENDS

Coffee is always evolving, and new ways of serving and savoring this drink are constantly being cooked up. Here are just a few fun examples to try (if you haven't already).

Nitro coffee

As if cold brew wasn't a big enough trend, nitro coffee has become just as ubiquitous. By infusing cold brew with nitrogen gas, you'll produce a velvety texture and the foam head of a Guinness, along with a naturally sweet taste without sugar or cream. To re-create this magic at home, all you need is a whipped cream dispenser equipped with a nitrogen charger—both can be ordered online.

Butter coffee

Also known as Bulletproof coffee, butter coffee allegedly suppresses hunger, sharpens mental acuity, and smooths out the caffeine jolt of coffee. Start with a cup of black coffee, add 1–2 tablespoons of grass-fed butter and 1–2 tablespoons of coconut oil, and blend to a latte-like consistency.

Coffee spritzers

Given the popularity of sparkling water, it's not surprising that coffee is being given a little sparkle of its own. These call for one part cold-brew concentrate to two parts sparkling water, served over ice. Experiment with different water flavors to give your fizzy coffee a fruity twist.

Oat milk in coffee

Oat milk was developed in the 1990s and its popularity has skyrocketed in the past couple of years—all thanks to coffeeshops. Of the many plant-based dairy alternatives, baristas around the world extol its taste and texture, noting that it froths just as nicely as cow's milk. Oat milk is also much more sustainable than traditional dairy and other nondairy options, ensuring that this coffee craze is here to stay.

Whipped coffee

One of the latest trends to take the world by storm is whipped coffee—also known as dalgona coffee in South Korea and desi coffee in India. Combine equal parts instant coffee, sugar, and water (hot or cold), beating the mixture using a whisk or hand mixer. If mixing by hand, be prepared to spend several minutes on this task—or take turns with a friend to give your arms a break. Once the mixture is fluffy and caramel colored, spoon over milk; add ice if you want your whipped coffee sweet and cool.

A SIMPLE RECIPE FOR BISCOTTI

Also known as *cantucci* in Italy, biscotti are traditional Italian cookies typically flavored with anise or almonds. From the Latin word *biscoctus*, meaning "twice cooked," biscotti are baked twice, which gives them the hard, crunchy texture that seems made for dunking in our morning coffee. This recipe makes 3–4 dozen cookies; if stored properly in an airtight container, biscotti keep and freeze well.

The best part is how easily biscotti can be customized with different flavors and ingredients. Experiment with adding chopped nuts, dried fruit, spices, or citrus zest. Drizzle cooled biscotti with melted chocolate for extra flair and sweetness.

Ingredients

- 1 cup granulated sugar
- 3 eggs
- ½ cup vegetable oil
- 1 tablespoon almond, anise, or vanilla extract
- 3¼ cups all-purpose flour
- 1 tablespoon baking powder

Directions

Preheat your oven to 375°F (190°C) and line a baking sheet with parchment paper. In a mixing bowl or the bowl of a stand mixer, combine the sugar, eggs, oil, and extract. Beat the mixture until well-blended. In another bowl, whisk the flour and baking powder together, and then add them to the egg mixture, stirring until incorporated.

Pour the dough onto the prepared baking sheet. Divide into halves and shape each piece into a flat log about ½ inch thick. The logs should be roughly the same size, so they cook evenly, and spaced a few inches apart (the dough will expand during baking). Bake the logs for 25–30 minutes. When they are golden brown, remove them from the oven (keep the oven on) and let cool on the baking sheet for about 20 minutes.

When they are cool to the touch, use a serrated knife to cut the logs crosswise into diagonal slices about ½ inch thick. Lay the slices on their cut side onto the baking sheet and return them to the oven for the second baking. Bake the slices for 6–10 minutes on each side, or until they're dry, crispy, and golden brown.

RESOURCES

Ethical Coffee Guide

Like fast fashion, the world of commodity coffee prioritizes profit over people. Here are a few things to look for to ensure that your coffee is ethical and environmentally friendly.

Direct trade: This refers to roasters who source high-quality beans directly from growers and pay them higher prices, instead of using importers or intermediaries. No official certifications for direct-trade coffee currently exist; look for small-batch roasters who visit coffee farms and have long-term relationships with growers. Specialty roasters such as Counter Culture publish annual transparency reports.

Shade grown: Better-quality coffee is also better for the environment. "Shade-grown" means the coffee was grown beneath a canopy of trees and foliage. These trees help prevent erosion, replenish the soil, retain water, and absorb carbon dioxide.

Bird friendly: Shade trees also support biodiversity by providing a habitat for native and migratory birds (who in turn provide natural pest control). The Smithsonian Migratory Bird Center has developed the Bird-Friendly coffee certification—considered the gold standard, and it's certified organic, too.

How to Find and Buy Specialty Coffee

Making delicious coffee at home all starts with using freshly roasted, high-quality beans—here's a quick primer on what to look for in specialty coffee and how to find it.

What to look for in specialty coffee:

Whole beans: Given what we know about how quickly ground coffee loses freshness, whole beans are a must. And be sure your beans are arabica, not robusta.

Traceability: Whether it's a single-origin coffee or a blend, specialty roasters typically state the origin on the label (or in the listing, if you're buying online). Look for details such as the producing country and region, harvest date, processing method, and even the name of the producer—a good sign that the roaster engages in direct trade (see opposite).

Roast date: The window of freshness for coffee beans is 2 to 3 weeks after roasting, so look for the roast date, instead of a "best by" expiration date; specialty brands typically note this date on their bags of beans.

Where to find specialty coffee:

Local: Skip your supermarket's coffee aisle and instead seek out nearby roasters and cafés, which often stock quality whole-bean coffee.

Online: If you don't have a local roaster, leading specialty roasters such as Intelligentsia and Blue Bottle Coffee sell their coffees online (the latter ships within 24 hours of roasting) and offer subscriptions as well.

FURTHER READING

For brewing tips:

- *The Blue Bottle Craft of Coffee: Growing, Roasting, and Drinking, with Recipes*
  by James Freeman, Caitlin Freeman, and Tara Duggan

- *Brew: Better Coffee at Home*
  by Brian W. Jones

- *Craft Coffee: A Manual*
  by Jessica Easto, with Andreas Willhoff

For general knowledge:

- *The Coffee Dictionary: An A–Z of Coffee, From Growing and Roasting to Brewing and Tasting*
  by Maxwell Colonna-Dashwood

- *The New Rules of Coffee: A Modern Guide for Everyone*
  by Jordan Michelman and Zachary Carlsen

For history and origins:

- *Uncommon Grounds: The History of Coffee and How It Transformed the World*
  by Mark Pendergrast

- *The World Atlas of Coffee*
  by James Hoffmann

ACKNOWLEDGMENTS

"To do good work one must eat well,
be well housed . . . and drink one's
coffee in peace."

—**Vincent van Gogh,** 19th-century Dutch painter

While I certainly agree with Van Gogh, I have to add one more requirement for doing good work: one must have a great team. For the chance to work on our second book together, I'm grateful to Jhanteigh Kupihea, Jane Morley, Rebecca Gyllenhaal, Mary Ellen Wilson, and the entire team at Quirk Books, as well as to illustrator Lucy Engelman for bringing the book to life visually.

I am especially grateful to my agent Rachel Sussman, cofounder of Chalberg & Sussman, and Veronica Leyton, owner of The Lab Coffee Roasters in Montevideo, Uruguay, for sharing her incredible knowledge and passion for coffee with me (not to mention delicious espresso drinks!).

Finally, thank you to my wonderful friends and family for their continued belief and support—in particular, my parents, Rob and Janell; my siblings, Brooke and Grant; and my husband, José, who may not share my love for coffee but is always right there with me in every project I'm a part of.